# CHOICES IN LITTLE ROCK

FACING
HISTORY &
OURSELVES

**Facing History and Ourselves** is an international educational and professional development organization whose mission is to use lessons of history to challenge teachers and their students to stand up to bigotry and hate. For more information about Facing History and Ourselves, please visit our website at www.facinghistory.org.

## Acknowledgments

**Facing History and Ourselves** would like to offer special thanks to The Yawkey Foundation for their support of *Choices in Little Rock*.

**Facing History and Ourselves** would like to acknowledge the valuable assistance it received from the Boston Public Schools in creating *Choices in Little Rock*. We are particularly appreciative of the team that consulted on the development of the unit under the leadership of Sidney W. Smith, Director, Curriculum and Instructional Practices, and Judith Berkowitz, Ed.D., Project Director for Teaching American History.

Patricia Artis, history coach
Magda Donis, language acquisitions coach
Meira Levinson, Ph.D., teacher, McCormack Middle School
Kris Taylor, history coach
Mark Taylor, teacher, King Middle School

**Facing History and Ourselves** would also like to offer special thanks to the Boston Public School teachers who piloted the unit and provided valuable suggestions for its improvement.

Constance Breeden, teacher, Irving Middle School
Saundra Coaxum, teacher, Edison Middle School
Gary Fisher, teacher, Timilty Middle School
Adam Gibbons, teacher, Lyndon School
Meghan Hendrickson, history coach, former teacher, Dearborn Middle School
Wayne Martin, Edwards Middle School
Peter Wolf, Curley Middle School

**Facing History and Ourselves** values the efforts of its staff in producing and implementing the unit. We are grateful to Margot Strom, Marc Skvirsky, Jennifer Jones Clark, Fran Colletti, Phyllis Goldstein, Jimmie Jones, Melinda Jones-Rhoades, Tracy O'Brien, Jenifer Snow, Jocelyn Stanton, Chris Stokes, and Adam Strom.

**Design:** Carter Halliday Associates
www.carterhalliday.com

Last updated December 2021.

ISBN-13: 978-0-9798440-5-8

# CONTENTS

## Introduction

*Choices in Little Rock* is a teaching unit that focuses on efforts to desegregate Central High School in Little Rock, Arkansas, in 1957 — efforts that resulted in a crisis that historian Taylor Branch once described as "the most severe test of the Constitution since the Civil War." The unit explores civic choices — the decisions people make as citizens in a democracy. Those decisions, both then and now, reveal that democracy is not a product but a work in progress, a work that is shaped in every generation by the choices that we make about ourselves and others. Although those choices may not seem important at the time, little by little, they define an individual, delineate a community, and ultimately distinguish a nation. Those choices build on the work of earlier generations and leave legacies for those to come.

Too often, discussions of civic responsibilities focus almost exclusively on voting. Although important, it is just one aspect of citizenship. Citizens influence their leaders and shape events in a wide variety of ways. The ballot box is only a part of the story. In *Choices in Little Rock*, students consider how ordinary people shape abstract ideas like the balance of power and federalism. The story is told through court decisions, political speeches, telegrams, letters, memoirs, interviews, and news reports. It is a story that teaches many lessons about race and racism as well as civic engagement. At the 40th anniversary of the crisis, President Bill Clinton listed some of those lessons in a speech he gave at Central High School:

> Well, 40 years later we know that we all benefit, all of us, when we learn together, work together and come together. That is, after all, what it means to be an American. Forty years later, we know, notwithstanding some cynics, that all our children can learn, and this school proves it.
>
> Forty years later, we know when the Constitutional rights of our citizens are threatened, the national government must guarantee them. Talk is fine, but when they are threatened, you need strong laws, faithfully enforced, and upheld by independent courts.
>
> Forty years later we know there are still more doors to be opened, doors to be opened wider, doors we have to keep from being shut again now.
>
> Forty years later we know freedom and equality cannot be realized without responsibility for self, family and the duties of citizenship, or without a commitment to building a community of shared destiny, and a genuine sense of belonging.
>
> Forty years later, we know the question of race is more complex and more important than ever, embracing no longer just blacks and whites, or blacks and whites and Hispanics and Native Americans, but now people from all parts of the earth coming here to redeem the promise of America.
>
> Forty years later, frankly, we know we are bound to come back where we started. After all the weary years and silent tears, after all the stony roads and bitter rides, the question of race is, in the end, still an affair of the heart.
>
> But...if these are lessons, what do we have to do? First, we must all reconcile. Then, we must all face the facts of today, and finally, we must act.

## Scope and Sequence

*Choices in Little Rock* can be used to enhance or deepen a civics, government, history, or literature course. Although the unit builds from one part to the next, activities and readings can be used independently or adapted to the needs of a particular class or curriculum.

The unit is divided into five parts:

- Part 1 introduces the concepts central to the unit — identity, race, prejudice, racism, and choice — by exploring the relationship between an individual and society. Students consider how identity can shape the choices people make about themselves and others.
- Part 2 provides the historical context in which the crisis in Little Rock occurred. The lessons in Part 2 trace the history of segregation in the United States and its social, legal, and political consequences.
- Part 3 begins the case study by examining the decisions that people in Little Rock and elsewhere made in response to *Brown v. Board of Education* during the 1957–1958 school year. Those decisions had consequences for the nation as well as the city of Little Rock and the state of Arkansas.
- Part 4 completes the case study by focusing on the 1958–1959 school year. That year, people in Little Rock had their first opportunity to vote on desegregation. In their first vote, they chose to close all public high schools in the city rather than allow integration. The schools remained closed until the fall of 1959 as voters considered and reconsidered earlier decisions.
- Part 5 explores the legacies of the *Brown* decision in Little Rock and elsewhere by examining the consequences of the choices made people over 50 years ago. The culminating activity for the unit is the creation of a project that highlights what students have learned from the crisis in Little Rock and the work that remains to be done.

## Organization

Each lesson in *Choices in Little Rock* explores a central question and related ideas. Each also develops and reinforces a working understanding of the U.S. system of government and teaches, reinforces, or extends a variety of skills central to citizenship in a democracy.

Every lesson begins with an activity called "Getting Started" that relates the lesson to its central question, ideas, and events featured in previous lessons, or students' prior experiences. Each lesson also contains:

- Background information that places key concepts or events in perspective.
- Interactive activities based on a variety of primary sources, including photographs, archival film footage, eyewitness accounts, telegrams, speeches, and diaries, that deepen understanding of key concepts and ideas. Many of these activities are designed to help students become thoughtful participants in class discussions and debates.

- Suggestions for discussion and writing assignments that deepen comprehension and explore events from more than one point of view.
- Packets of primary sources and a variety of reproducibles that build comprehension and promote speaking, listening, and critical thinking skills.

The structure of the lessons allows teachers to choose the activities and materials that meet the needs of their students and address course objectives. If taught from start to finish, the unit will take about six weeks to complete. The unit can be taught in less time by adapting activities and selecting materials most relevant to course objectives, the time available, and the interests of students. The unit can also be expanded by using one or more of the suggestions provided under Related Resources.

## Related Resources

### Facing History Resources

*Choosing to Participate.* (A Guide to the Choosing to Participate Exhibition)
*Holocaust and Human Behavior.*
*Race and Membership in American History: The Eugenics Movement.*

### Books

Bates, Daisy. *The Long Shadow of Little Rock.* Reprint edition. University of Arkansas Press, 1987. An account by the president of the Arkansas chapter of the NAACP in 1957, the woman who helped the African American students and their parents stand firm.

Beals, Melba Patillo. *Warriors Don't Cry.* Pocket Books, 1994, 1995. An account by one of the African American students who desegregated Central High School. (Teacher's Guide available from Facing History and Ourselves)

Carson, Clayborne, et al., eds. *The Eyes on the Prize Civil Rights Reader: Documents, Speeches, and Firsthand Accounts from the Black Freedom Struggle, 1954–1990.* Penguin, 1991. Includes materials on the crisis in Little Rock.

Freyer, Tony. *The Little Rock Crisis: A Constitutional Interpretation.* Greenwood Press, 1984. A reference book for teachers.

Hampton, Henry, et. al. *Voices of Freedom: An Oral History of the Civil Rights Movement from the 1950s through the 1980s.* Bantam Books, 1990.

Huckaby, Elizabeth. *Crisis at Central High: Little Rock, 1957–58.* Louisiana State University Press, 1980. An account by the vice principal of the school.

Levine, Ellen. *Freedom's Children: Young Civil Rights Activists Tell Their Own Stories.* Putnam, 1993.

Murphy, Sara Alderman. *Breaking the Silence: Little Rock's Women's Emergency Committee to Open Our Schools.* University of Arkansas Press, 1997. A participant's account of the 1958–1959 school year in Little Rock.

Patterson, Charles. *The Civil Rights Movement.* Facts on File, 1995. Primary sources including interviews with people in Little Rock.

## Videos

*Eye of the Storm.* Social Studies School Service. An account of an experiment on discrimination in a third-grade classroom in Iowa.*

*Eyes on the Prize: America's Civil Rights Years*, tape 2, "Fighting Back." PBS Video. An account of the crisis in Little Rock based on archival footage.*

*The Hangman.* CRM Films. A 12-minute animated film that sparks discussion of the role of bystanders and raises questions about individual responsibility.

*Hoxie: The First Stand.* New York Cinema Guild. A 56-minute documentary about a small town in Arkansas that voluntarily desegregated its schools in 1955. The response to the decision played a role in events in Little Rock.

*The Road to Brown.* California Newsreel. An account of the legal campaign against segregation from *Plessey v. Ferguson* in 1806 to *Brown v. Board of Education* in 1954.*

*The Second American Revolution*, Part 2. PBS Video. An account of the struggle for civil rights.*

For additional videos that address issues of race, particularly in education, contact the Facing History Resource Center (library@facing.org) or download the *Guide to Audio Visual Resources* at www.facinghistory.org.

Videos followed by an asterisk (*) are the focus of one or more lessons.

## Websites

Facing History and Ourselves: http://www.facinghistory.org.

40th Anniversary of the Crisis at Central High School: http://www.centralhigh57.org.

Little Rock Crisis: Eisenhower Archives:
http://www.eisenhower.archives.gov/dl/LittleRock/littlerockdocuments.

Little Rock, 1957: Pages from History The Central High Crisis:
http://www.ardemgaz.com/prev/central.

# PART 1: **Individual and Society**

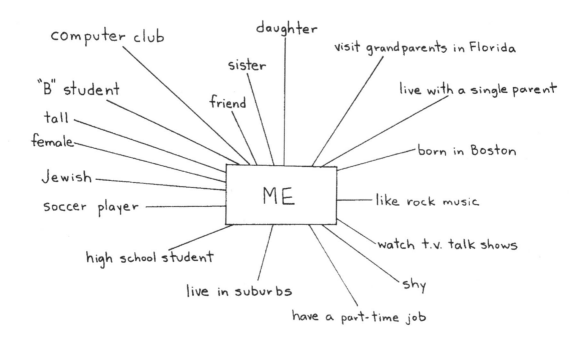

computer club

"B" student

tall

female

Jewish

soccer player

daughter

sister

friend

visit grandparents in Florida

live with a single parent

born in Boston

ME

like rock music

watch t.v. talk shows

shy

high school student

live in suburbs

have a part-time job

# PART 1: Individual and Society

## Central Questions
- How does our identity shape the way we see ourselves and others?
- To what extent does our identity influence the choices we make?

## Student Outcomes
- Understands the relationship between identity and decision making
- Recognizes the ways identity influences perception of self and others
- Compares and contrasts various perspectives
- Develops a working understanding of such key concepts as identity, stereotypes, and race
- Uses logic and reason to defend a point of view

## Teaching Focus
The four lessons in Part 1 introduce the concepts central to this unit — identity, race, prejudice, and racism — by exploring the relationship between an individual and society. Students will consider how identity can shape the choices people make about themselves and others.

# LESSON 1: Who Are We?

**Central Question:** How does our identity shape the way we see ourselves and others?

## Getting Started

Explain to students that the question "Who are you?" is one that almost everyone has been asked at one time or another. In answering, we define ourselves. Our identity is a combination of many things. It includes the labels others place on us, as well as the words and phrases we use to describe ourselves. Gender, ethnicity, religion, occupation, and physical characteristics all contribute to our identity. So do ties to a particular neighborhood, school, community, or nation. Our values and beliefs are also a part of who we are as individuals, as are the experiences that have shaped our lives.

## Background Information

Most people view identity as a combination of many factors, including physical traits, values and beliefs, and social ties — connections to a family, an ethnic group, a community, or a nation. Although the ways we define ourselves — and others — seem ordinary, those definitions can have powerful and long-lasting consequences. "When we identify one thing as unlike the others," observes Martha Minow, a legal scholar, "we are dividing the world; we use our language to exclude, to distinguish — to discriminate." She goes on to say:

> Of course, there are "real differences" in the world; each person differs in countless ways from each other person. But when we simplify and sort, we focus on some traits rather than others, and we assign consequences to the presence and absence of the traits we make significant. We ask, "What's the new baby?" — and we expect as an answer, boy or girl. That answer, for most of history, has spelled consequences for the roles and opportunities available to that individual.[1]

## Activity: Creating an Identity Box

One way to help students think about their identity is by asking them to create an identity box. To model the process, create your own identity box (or paper bag). It might focus on who you are today or who you were as a teen. On the outside of a cardboard box or brown paper bag write words that others might use to describe you now or then. Inside the box or bag place pictures of people important in your life and brief descriptions of events that have shaped who you are or mementos of those experiences. Share one or two items from inside and outside of the box with the class. Be sure to explain the significance of each item by telling how it helped to influence your identity.

---

[1] Martha Minow, *Making All the Difference: Inclusion, Exclusion and American Law*. Cornell University Press, 1990, p.3.

Ask students to use a paper bag or a cardboard box to create their own identity box. On the outside, ask them to write the words others might use to describe them. On the inside, ask them to place pictures, brief descriptions, or mementoes of individuals or experiences that are important to their identity. When the boxes are complete, invite students to share one or two items from the inside or outside of their box with a partner.

### Activity: Identifying Perspective in a Personal Essay

After students have shared their boxes, distribute **Reproducible 1.1.** Explain to students that it contains an essay written by a high school student in response to the question "Who are you?" After students have read the essay and discussed the questions at the end of the essay with a partner, have partners work together to create an identity box or bag for Jennifer Wang. What words and phrases does she use to describe herself? What experiences have shaped her identity? Ask students to place these words and phrases inside the box. On the outside, have them write the labels that others place on her.

### Activity: Comparing and Contrasting Identity Boxes

Ask partners to compare the box they created for Jennifer Wang with their own boxes. What do they have in common with Jennifer and with one another? In what ways is each box unique? Encourage students to add to their identity boxes or bags as the unit progresses.

### Discussion Suggestions

- What does Jennifer mean when she asks, "Who or what determines when a person starts feeling American, and stops feeling Chinese?" How would you answer her question?
- Why do you think Jennifer wonders, "Am I Chinese? Am I American? Or am I some unholy mixture of both, doomed to stay torn between the two?"
- How do the questions Jennifer asks apply to you and the way you define your identity?

### Writing Suggestions

- Introduce yourself in much the way Jennifer Wang introduced herself. What two words does she believe best describe her identity? What words or phrases describe who you are?
- What questions do you have about your identity? How are they similar to Jennifer's questions? How do you account for differences?

## "Orientation Day"

At the age of 7, Jennifer Wang came to the United States from Beijing, China, with her family. At 17, she wrote an essay entitled "Orientation Day" in response to a familiar experience: introducing oneself to a group of strangers. Wang writes in part:

Something about myself? How do I summarize, in thirty seconds, everything, which adds up and equals a neat little bundle called Me? How do I present myself in a user-friendly format, complete with "Help" buttons and batteries? Who am I, and why do I matter to any of you?

First of all, I am a girl who wandered the aisles of Toys "R" Us for two hours, hunting in vain for a doll with a yellowish skin tone. I am a girl who sat on the cold bathroom floor at seven in the morning, cutting out the eyes of Caucasian models in magazines, trying to fit them on my face. I am the girl who loved [newscaster] Connie Chung because she was Asian, and I'm also the girl who hated Connie Chung because she wasn't Asian enough....

During that time I also first heard the term *chink*, and I wondered why people were calling me "a narrow opening, usually in a wall." People expected me to love studying and to enjoy sitting in my room memorizing facts for days and days.

While I was growing up, I did not understand what it meant to be "Chinese" or "American." Do these terms link only to citizenship? Do they suggest that people fit the profile of either "typical" Chinese or "typical" Americans? And who or what determines when a person starts feeling American, and stops feeling Chinese? ...

I am still not a citizen of the United States of America, this great nation, which is hailed as the destination for generations of people, the promised land for millions. I flee at the mere hint of teenybopper music. I stare blankly at my friends when they mention the 1980s or share stories of their parents as hippies. And I hate baseball.

The question lingers: Am I Chinese? Am I American? Or am I some unholy mixture of both, doomed to stay torn between the two?

I don't know if I'll ever find the answers. Meanwhile, it's my turn to introduce myself.... I stand up and say, "My name is Jennifer Wang," and then I sit back down. There are no other words that define me as well as those do. No others show me being stretched between two very different cultures and places — the "Jennifer" clashing with the "Wang," the "Wang" fighting with the "Jennifer."*

CONTINUED

---

* Jennifer Wang, "Orientation Day" [pp. 199–200] from Vickie Nam, *Yell-Oh Girls!* Copyright © 2001 by Vickie Nam. Reprinted by permission of HarperCollins Publishers.

**Reproducible 1.1**
**Page 2 of 2**

1.  Underline the words and phrases that Jennifer uses to describe herself.

2.  Based on her description of herself, what words or phrases would you use to describe Jennifer?

3.  How does being Chinese shape Jennifer's identity?

4.  How does being American shape her identity?

5.  What experiences does Jennifer identify as important to who she is and how she sees herself? Which of those experiences do you think has had the greatest impact on her identity?

6.  What experiences are important to who you are and how you see yourself? Which of those experiences has had the greatest impact on your identity?

# LESSON 2: Why "Little Things Are Big"

**Central Question:** To what extent does our identity influence the choices we make?

## Getting Started

Discuss the meaning of the word *stereotype*. How is it like a first impression? How does it differ from a first impression? Then have students describe their own experiences with stereotyping or those of someone they know or have read about. Ask them to describe an incident involving stereotyping. How did the person who was stereotyped react?

## Background Information

Psychologist Deborah Tannen writes, "We all know we are unique individuals but we tend to see others as representatives of groups. It's a natural tendency, since we must see the world in patterns in order to make sense of it; we wouldn't be able to deal with the daily onslaught of people and objects if we couldn't predict a lot about them and feel that we know who or what they are." Although Tannen considers it "natural" to generalize, she views stereotypes as offensive. A *stereotype* is more than a judgment about an individual based on the characteristics of a group. Stereotyping reduces individuals to categories.

## Activity: Taking a Stand

Distribute **Reproducible 1.2** and ask students to read the essay and answer the questions at the end of the reading. (If you would prefer to have your class listen to the story, go to www.facinghistory.org and click on "Choosing to Participate." Then locate the online exhibition and enter the section called "Little Things Are Big." Please keep in mind that the online version of the essay has been abridged and slightly simplified. It cannot be used in conjunction with Reproducible 1.2.) While the class reads or listens to "Little Things Are Big," post two signs at opposite ends of the classroom: one should read "Help" and the other "Don't help." When students have completed the reading and answered the questions, ask them to silently find a place to stand between the two signs. Explain that the closer they are to a sign, the more strongly they are showing their support for its message. Although students may feel certain of their position at the start of the activity, be sure they understand that they can change their place along the line if their opinion changes.

After everyone has lined up between the two signs, ask various students to explain why they have chosen their current position along the line. Encourage them to defend their stand with logic and reason. In calling on students, try to select those at each end of the spectrum, as well as those in the middle. Once three or four viewpoints have been heard, allow time for moves before continuing. After everyone has been heard and allowed to move if they so choose, ask students what aspects of their own identity shaped their opinion. To what extent do they think stereotypes may have influenced the choice they made?

**Activity: Evaluating a Decision**

Share the decision that Jesus Colon actually made by reading aloud the end of the essay.

> It was a long minute. I passed on by her as if I saw nothing. As if I was insensitive to her need. Like a rude animal walking on two legs, I just moved on, half running by the long subway platform, leaving the children and the valise and her with the baby on her arm. I took the steps of the long concrete stairs in twos until I reached the street above and the cold air slapped my warm face.
>
> This is what racism and prejudice … and official artificial divisions can do to people and to a nation!
>
> Perhaps the lady was not prejudiced after all. Or not prejudiced enough to scream at the coming of a Negro toward her in a solitary subway station a few hours past midnight.
>
> If you were not that prejudiced, I failed you, dear lady. I know that there is a chance in a million that you will read these lines. I am willing to take the millionth chance. If you were not that prejudiced, I failed you, lady. I failed you, children. I failed myself to myself.
>
> I buried my courtesy early on Memorial Day morning. But here is a promise that I made to myself here and now; if I am ever faced with an occasion like that again, I am going to offer my help regardless of how the offer is going to be received.
>
> Then I will have my courtesy with me again.[2]

Ask students what they think Colon meant when he wrote, "I buried my courtesy early on Memorial Day morning." What does his courtesy mean to him? How does he hope to regain it? To evaluate Colon's decision and why he regretted the choice he made, have students work with a partner to create a t-chart. In the first column, have the partners identify Colon's fears. In the second column, have them list his regrets. Ask partners to use their chart to answer the following questions:

- What was Colon's dilemma?
- How did the attitudes and values of others shape the choice he made?
- Did he make the right choice? Would your answer be the same if he were a white man? Would your answer change if the author were an African American woman?
- How did your own identity and the identity of your partner influence the way you evaluated Colon's decision?

---

[2] Jesus Colon, *A Puerto Rican in New York*. Mainstream, 1961.

**Activity: Tough Choices**

Ask students to write a paragraph about a tough choice they or someone they know made. Encourage them to choose a decision that involved stereotyping. The paragraph should explain why the decision was difficult to make, the factors that shaped the decision, and the effects of that decision. What lessons did students learn from this decision?

**Writing Suggestions**

- Who was the victim in Jesus Colon's story — Colon, the woman, or society?
- What did you find surprising or difficult to understand about Colon's decision? What did you find surprising about the way he viewed that decision?

## Little Things Are Big

In the 1950s, Jesus Colon had an unsettling experience during a late-night subway ride in New York City.

It was very late at night on the eve of Memorial Day. She came into the subway at the 34th Street Pennsylvania Station. I am still trying to remember how she managed to push herself in with a baby on her right arm, a [suitcase] in her left hand and two children, a boy and girl about three and five years old, trailing after her. She was a nice-looking white lady in her early twenties.

At Nevins Street, Brooklyn, we saw her preparing to get off at the next station — Atlantic Avenue — which happened to be the place where I too had to get off. Just as it was a problem for her to get on, it was going to a problem for her to get off the subway with two small children to be taken care of, a baby on her right arm, and a medium-sized [suitcase] in her left hand.

And there I was, also preparing to get off at Atlantic Avenue, with no bundles to take care of — not even the customary book under my arm, without which I feel that I am not completely dressed.

As the train was entering the Atlantic Avenue station, some white man stood up from his seat and helped her out, placing the children on the long, deserted platform. There were only two adult persons on the long platform some time after midnight on the evening of last Memorial Lesson.

I could perceive the steep, long concrete stairs going down to the Long Island Railroad or into the street. Should I offer my help as the American white man did at the subway door, placing the two children outside the subway car? Should I take care of the girl and the boy, take them by their hands until they reached the end of the steep, long concrete stairs of the Atlantic Avenue station?

Courtesy is a characteristic of the Puerto Rican. And here I was — a Puerto Rican hours past midnight, a valise, two white children and a white lady with a baby on her arm badly needing somebody to help her, at least until she descended the long concrete stairs.

But how could I, a Negro* and a Puerto Rican, approach this white lady, who very likely might have preconceived prejudices about Negroes and everybody with foreign accents, in a deserted subway station very late at night?

CONTINUED

---

* The word *Negro* was commonly used until the late 1960s to refer to an African American. Its use reflects the time period.

**Reproducible 1.2**
**Page 2 of 2**

What would she say? What would be the first reaction of this white American woman perhaps coming from a small town with a [suitcase], two children and a baby on her right arm? Would she say: "Yes, of course, you may help me." Or would she think that I was just trying to get too familiar? Or would she think worse than that perhaps? What would I do if she let out a scream as I went forward to offer my help?

Was I misjudging her? So many slanders are written every day in the daily press against the Negroes and Puerto Ricans. I hesitated for a long, long minute.*

1.      Underline the words or phrases that Jesus Colon uses to define his identity.

2.      If you were to create an identity box for Colon, what words would you place on the inside of the box?

3.      What words or phrases would you place outside the box?

4.      What do you think Jesus Colon should do? Be sure to list the reasons you think he should make that choice.

---

*Jesus Colon, *A Puerto Rican in New York*. Mainstream, 1961.

# LESSON 3: Why Differences Matter

## Central Questions

- How does our identity shape the way we see ourselves and others?
- To what extent does our identity influence the choices we make?

## Getting Started

Explain to students that after making his decision, Jesus Colon wrote with regret, "This is what racism and prejudice … and official artificial divisions can do to people and to a nation!" What did he mean? How do beliefs about differences in our society shape the way we see ourselves and others? How do they shape the way others see us? In the 1970s, during the Civil Rights Movement, Jane Elliott, a teacher in a small town in Iowa, decided to help her third graders understand how society can influence our beliefs about our own identity and the identities of our neighbors.

## Background Information

The word *prejudice* comes from the word *pre-judge*. We pre-judge when we have an opinion about a person solely because of a group to which that individual belongs. A prejudice has the following characteristics:

- It is based on real or imagined differences between groups.
- It attaches value to those differences in ways that falsely assume that one's own group is superior to others.
- It is generalized to include all members of a target group.

Not all prejudices result in discrimination. Discrimination occurs when prejudices are translated into action.

## Activity: Analyzing an Experiment

Before showing students the last 15 minutes of the film *The Eye of the Storm*, explain that the film was made in the 1970s and reflects the language used at that time. Jane Elliott initiated her experiment because of her concern with the way her students spoke of people they had never met. (Begin with the section titled "Tuesday Morning," which marks the start of Jane Elliott's experiment, and continue to the end of the film.) As soon as the video ends, ask students to use their journal or interactive student notebook to list what they learned from the program; what surprised them; what they found upsetting or disturbing; and questions that the program raised but did not answer.

In small groups, have students briefly discuss their observations about the film. Then ask them to decide:

- Who in the film determined which differences mattered?
- Who do you think decides in real life?
- What is the lesson Jane Elliott wanted her students to learn?
- What lesson did you learn from the film?

### Activity: Comparing and Contrasting Points of Views

Reproducible 1.3 tells of a choice a woman made about her identity. Divide the class into small groups and ask students to read her story and then discuss why Susie Phipps would spend $20,000 to change her birth certificate. Have the group also consider why the state of Louisiana had a way to officially determine a person's race. Then ask students to compare and contrast Jane Elliott's classroom experiment with Susie Phipps's story. In what ways are the two stories similar? What differences do you consider most striking?

### Writing Suggestions

- What would you like Jane Elliott's students to know about the way you and your friends think about differences? Who decides which differences matter today?
- Why would a tiny percentage of Black ancestry cause Susie Phipps to be considered African American, while her overwhelmingly white ancestry was ignored?
- If you were to create an identity box for Susie Phipps, what words, phrases, or experiences would you put inside the box? What labels would you place on the outside of the box?

**Reproducible 1.3**

# Things Are Not Always What They Seem

Sociologist Allan G. Johnson writes:

> Imagine that you apply for a copy of your birth certificate one day, and when you receive it, you discover that it lists your "race" as something other than what you and everyone else always considered it to be. You are Black, and the certificate says you are white; or you are white, and it says you are Black. How would you feel?
>
> This is exactly what happened in 1977 to Susie Guillory Phipps — a New Orleans resident who had always been white, both to herself and to everyone who encountered her. She had twice married white men, and her family album was filled with pictures of blue-eyed, white ancestors. The state of Louisiana, however, defined her as "colored."
>
> When she protested to state authorities, they carefully traced her ancestry back 222 years, and found that [one of her 64 great-great-great-great grandparents] was Black. Under Louisiana law, anyone whose ancestry was at least 3 percent Black was considered black. Thus, even with an ancestry 97 percent white, the state defined her as Black.
>
> Susie Phipps spent $20,000 to force Louisiana to change her birth certificate, and in 1983 Louisiana repealed the law.*

1.  How did Susie Phipps see herself? How did the state of Louisiana see her?

2.  Who should decide whether Susie Phipps or anyone else is African American or white?

3.  Why did Phipps go to court to change her birth certificate?

---

\* Allan G. Johnson, *Human Arrangements: An Introduction to Sociology.* Harcourt, Brace, 1986, p.353.

# LESSON 4: Race and Identity

## Central Questions

- How does race shape the way we see ourselves and others?
- To what extent do our ideas about race influence the choices we make?

## Getting Started

Remind students that race is one part of a person's identity. Yet Susie Phipps considered it so important that she spent $20,000 trying to change the way Louisiana determined her race. What is *race*? What does Phipps's legal battle suggest about its importance in the United States in the 1970s? How important is your race to your identity? If students have difficulty expressing their ideas about race, you may want to read aloud to them from picture books about race created for young children. A good example is *Let's Talk about Race* written by Julius Lester and illustrated by Karen Barbour (HarperCollins, 2005). Lester relates his ideas about race to his own identity.

## Background Information

In 1997, the American Anthropological Association (AAA) wrote a statement on race:
> Physical variations in the human species have no meaning except the social [meanings] that humans put on them. Today, scholars in many fields argue that race as it is understood in the USA was a social mechanism invented during the 18th century to refer to those populations brought together in colonial America: the English and other European settlers, the conquered Indian peoples, and those peoples of Africa brought to provide slave labor.

The report notes that in the early 1800s slaveholders justified slavery by magnifying differences among Europeans, Africans, and American Indians and insisting that those differences were "God-given." A number of scientists incorporated these mistaken notions about human differences into their research. Eventually these myths about race spread to other areas of the world where they "became a strategy for dividing, ranking and controlling colonized people." But racist thinking was not limited to the "colonial situation."

The report goes on to say:
> In the latter part of the 19th century, [race] was employed by Europeans to rank one another and to justify social, economic, and political inequalities among their peoples. During World War II, the Nazis under Adolf Hitler enjoined the expanded ideology of race and racial differences and took them to a logical end: the extermination of 11 million people of "inferior races"… and other unspeakable brutalities of the Holocaust.

Race thus evolved as a world view, a body of prejudgments that distorts our ideas about human differences and group behavior.... Racial myths bear no relationship to the reality of human capabilities or behavior. Scientists today find that reliance on such folk beliefs about human difference in research has led to countless errors.[3]

In short, race is skin deep. Yet, writes anthropologist Jared Diamond, "Most people regard the existence of race as obvious, a matter of common sense even though 'science often violates simple common sense.'" He explains:

Our eyes tell us that the Earth is flat, that the sun revolves around the Earth, and that we humans are not animals. But we now ignore that evidence of our senses. We have learned that our planet is in fact round and revolves around the sun, and that humans are slightly modified chimpanzees. The reality of human races is another commonsense "truth" destined to follow the flat Earth into oblivion.[4]

### Activity: Analyzing Ideas about Race and Racism

Write the word *race* on the board and draw a circle around it. Ask students to create a web by listing the words, phrases, or ideas they associate with the word. (If you read Lester's book to the class, students may wish to include his ideas as well.) Explain to students that many scholars, scientists, and writers have also thought about the word and its meaning. Distribute **Reproducible 1.4** and ask students to read the definitions. What do they add to our understanding of race? Point out that the authors of the first definition of race on the reproducible has put into **bold** key phrases and ideas. Ask students to work with a partner and underline key phrases and ideas in the other definitions. Have the class add those understandings to their web as well.

After students have read and discussed their ideas about race, read aloud the following paragraph from *Let's Talk about Race.* Julius Lester writes:

Just as I am a story and you are a story and countries tell stories about themselves, race is a story, too. Whether you're black like me, or Asian, Hispanic, or white, each race has a story about itself. And that story is almost always the same:
"MY RACE IS BETTER THAN YOUR RACE."
Some stories are true. Some are not.
Those who say
"MY RACE IS BETTER THAN YOUR RACE"
are telling a story that is not true.[5]

[4] "The American Anthropological Association Preliminary Statement on Race." *Anthropology Newsletter,* April 1997, p.1.
[5] Jared Diamond, "Race without Color". *Discover,* November 1994, p. 82–89.
[6] Julius Lester, *Let's Talk about Race.* HarperCollins, 2005.

Ask students to use their web to explain the lesson Lester wants his readers to learn. Explain that those who say "My race is better than your race" believe in *racism*. Ask students to work in pairs to create a visual definition of racism. Post the definitions around the classroom and allow students time to look at one another's work. What do the pictures suggest about the meanings of both *race* and *racism*?

### Activity: Expressing a Point of View

Ask students to read **Reproducible 1.5** and then answer the questions at the end of the reading. Their answers should show an understanding of how identity shapes perception (questions 1 and 2), and how stereotypes are formed (question 3) and how they can be overcome (question 4).

### Writing Suggestions

Create working definitions of race and racism. A working definition begins with what a word or term means to you. Then add the meanings explored in your reading. Continue to add definitions as the unit continues.

**Reproducible 1.4**
**Page 1 of 2**

# The Meanings of Race

Read each definition of race and underline key phrases and ideas. You will use those phrases and ideas to create a web about race.

## Definition 1

### The Only Race Is the Human Race
### No Biological Basis for Race

New data from the mapping of the human genome reveal that all humans are incredibly similar — in fact, we are 99.9% genetically identical. **We are all members of one species,** *Homo sapiens.* Scientists have confirmed, as they long suspected, **that there is no genetic or biological basis for race.**

Genetic variation between people within the same "racial" group can be greater than the variation between people of two different groups. Many people of African descent are no more similar to other Africans than they are to Caucasians. Genetic distinctions between Asians and Caucasians are less pronounced than those between groups from, for example, parts of East and West Africa.

No matter how scientists today scrutinize a person's genes, they can't determine with certainty whether an individual is from one "racial" group or another. **Differences of culture and society** distinguish one group from another, but these distinctions are not rooted in biology.

*"Mapping the DNA sequence variation in the human genome holds the potential for promoting the fundamental unity of all mankind." —Dr. Harold P. Freeman*

(American Museum of Natural History, "The Genomic Revolution," 2001 exhibition.)

## Definition 2

In 1997, the American Anthropological Association (AAA) issued a statement summarizing its own research and the research of others on race. After noting that race has no scientific meaning and that research based on racial categories has resulted in "countless errors," the organization concluded that race is a social invention — "a worldview, a body of pre-judgments that distorts our ideas about human differences and group behavior." The AAA noted, "At the end of the 20th century, we now understand that human behavior is learned, conditioned into infants beginning at birth and always subject to modification and change."

CONTINUED

**Reproducible 1.4**
**Page 2 of 2**

## Definition 3

*Webster's Ninth New Collegiate Dictionary*

**race** *n* a division of mankind possessing traits that are transmissible by descent and sufficient to characterize it as a distinct human type

## Definition 4

Poet Lori Tsang:

> Race is the myth upon which the reality of racism is based, the wild card the racist always keeps up his sleeve. The racist has the power to determine whether the card will be a diamond or spade, whether a Chinese is black or white. Like water, race takes on the shape of whatever contains it — whatever culture, social structure, political system. But like water, it slips through your fingers when you try to hold it.*

---

*Quoted in Claudine Chiawei O'Hearn, ed., *Half and Half.* Pantheon Books, 1998, pp. 209–210.

**Reproducible 1.5**

# "Those Who Don't"

In *House on Mango Street*, Sandra Cisneros writes:

> Those who don't know any better come into our neighborhood scared. They think we're dangerous. They think we will attack them with shiny knives. They are stupid people who are lost and got here by mistake.
>
> But we aren't afraid. We know the guy with the crooked eye is Davy the Baby's brother, and the tall one next to him in the straw brim, that's Rosa's Eddie V., and the big one that looks like a dumb grown man, he's Fat Boy, though he's not fat anymore nor a boy.
>
> All brown all around, we are safe. But watch us drive into a neighborhood of another color and our knees go shakity-shake and our car windows get rolled up tight and our eyes look straight. Yeah. That is how it goes and goes.*

1.    List the stereotypes that *they* have of us.

2.    List the stereotypes that *we* have of *them*.

3.    Where does the author think the stereotypes she describes come from?
      Where do you think they come from?

4.    Write a paragraph explaining what can be done to stop stereotyping.
      Give your opinion in the first sentence. The sentences that follow should
      provide an argument in support of your opinion.

---

* From *House on Mango Street*. Copyright © Sandra Cisneros, 1984. Published in the United States by Vintage Books, a division of Random House, Inc., New York. Reprinted by persion of Susan Bergholz Literary Series, New York.

# PART 2: Dividing a Nation
## Segregation and Its Consequences

# PART 2: Dividing a Nation
# Segregation and Its Consequences

## Central Questions

- What are the consequences of dividing people by race?
- How can individuals and groups in a democracy organize to correct injustices?

## Student Outcomes

- Interprets constitutional amendments and analyzes court decisions based on those amendments
- Develops a working definition of such key concepts as racism and segregation
- Examines primary sources for insights into a time period
- Traces a strategy to overturn segregation through the nation's court system

## Teaching Focus

The four lessons in Part 2 provide an historical context for understanding the crisis in Little Rock, Arkansas, in 1957. The lessons trace the history of segregation in the United States and its social, legal, and political consequences

# LESSON 1: The Legacies of Segregation

**Central Question:** What are the consequences of dividing people by race?

### Getting Started

Explain that until the 1960s and 1970s, many states had laws that required segregation — the required separation of people by race. Although those laws no longer exist, their legacy still shapes the way many people view themselves and others. Ask students what they know about *segregation*. How is *segregation* related to *race* and *racism*? Record their ideas on the board.

### Background Information

In the nineteenth century, many Americans came to believe that some races are superior to others. Few questioned that idea. After all, racist ideas were taught in schools and even universities, preached from pulpits, and reinforced in books, magazines, and newspapers. After surveying the leading publications in the middle of the nineteenth century, historian Reginald Horsman notes, "One did not have to read obscure books to know that the Caucasians were innately superior, and that they were responsible for civilization in the world, or to know that inferior races were destined to be overwhelmed or even to disappear. These ideas permeated the main American periodicals and in the second half of the [nineteenth century] formed part of the accepted truth of America's schoolbooks." They also shaped the way Americans defined citizenship.

Immediately after the American Revolution (1776–1783), only three states — Virginia, South Carolina, and Georgia — allowed only white men to vote. Until 1800, no northern state limited suffrage on the basis of race. After 1800, however, every state that entered the Union, with the exception of Maine, placed restrictions on the right of African Americans to vote. States that had long permitted Black Americans to vote now narrowed or removed that right entirely. In 1821, for example, New Yorkers wrote a new constitution. It no longer required that white male citizens own property in order to vote. At the same time, it *raised* the property requirement for Black citizens to $250, a sum beyond the reach of almost all of the state's Black voters at that time. By the late 1850s, Black Americans could vote on the same basis as whites in only five states — all of them in New England.

In 1857, the language of exclusion reached the U.S. Supreme Court. In the *Dred Scott* decision, Chief Justice Roger B. Taney ruled that Black Americans "had no rights which the white man was bound to respect." The American people, Taney argued, constituted a "political family" restricted to whites. Although slavery was abolished in 1865, the amendment to the Constitution did not end racism. In fact, in the late 1800s and early 1900s, the number of state and federal laws that kept the races apart increased sharply. Historian Lerone Bennett, Jr., likens the system of segregation that divided Black and white Americans during those years to "a wall." That wall did not go up in a single day. It was built, he writes, "brick by brick, bill by bill, fear by fear." Long after that wall came down in the 1970s, the legacies of decades of separation remained.

## Activity: Defining Segregation

Explain to students that they are about to read a description of segregation by someone who experienced it. Distribute **Reproducible 2.1** to half the class and **Reproducible 2.2** to the other half of the class. Ask students to read the essay and answer the questions that follow it.

When students have completed the assignment, divide the class into pairs in such a way that one partner has read Reproducible 2.1 and the other Reproducible 2.2. Have partners share what they learned about segregation from their reading. Ask each pair to create a working definition of *segregation* based on the two readings. Encourage students to share their definitions with the class. How are the definitions similar? What differences seem to be most striking? How do these definitions relate to the word *race*? How do they relate to the word *racism*?

## Activity: Understanding the Legacies of Segregation

Ask partners to imagine a meeting between Lisa Delpit and Daniel Dyer. Where might they meet? What do students think the two would have to say to each another? Have each pair write a dialogue for such a conversation. Ask students to establish the place and the year in which the dialogue takes place.

Invite pairs to act out their dialogue for the class. After hearing a few, have students consider what the conversations have in common. What do they add to our understanding of the meaning of the term *segregation*? What do they add to our understanding of the legacies of *segregation*?

## Activity: Beyond Black and White

Remind students that not everyone in the United States fits neatly into two categories — one Black and the other white. Where do Asian Americans fit? Are Latinos Black or white? In which category would you place Native Americans? To help students deepen their understanding of segregation, share the following story:

> Lori Tsang is a Chinese American. In the 1950s, her aunt and uncle took a trip across the United States. Aware of segregation laws in the South, they were careful to sit at the back of buses and in separate compartments on trains. In one southern city, however, the bus driver stopped the bus and ordered them to move to the front to sit with whites. Tsang says of the incident, "Race is the myth upon which the reality of racism is based, the wild card the racist always keeps up his sleeve. The racist has the power to determine whether the card will be a diamond or spade, whether a Chinese is black or white." [6]

Ask students what the story adds to their working definitions of *race* and *racism*. What does Tsang mean when she calls *race* a myth and *racism* a reality? How are the two related in her opinion? What does she mean when she says that "the racist has the power to determine whether...a Chinese is black or white"?

[6] Quoted in Claudine Chiawei O'Hearn, ed. *Half and Half.* Pantheon Books, 1998, pp. 209–210.

**Writing Suggestions**

- Describe your experiences with segregation and its legacies. What do those experiences add to your understanding of the term?
- How can we as individuals and as members of a community overcome the legacies of segregation? How have both Lisa Delpit and Daniel Dyer tried to overcome the past?

## Growing Up with Segregation

Lisa Delpit is an educator who grew up in Baton Rouge, Louisiana, at a time when police officers patrolled the street that separated the city's Black and white residents. Although that time in history has passed, her experiences continue to shape Delpit's views, including her hopes and fears for her child. In a letter to her daughter, Maya, Delpit writes:

As much as I think of you as my gift to the world, I am constantly made aware that there are those who see you otherwise.

Although you don't realize it yet, it is solely because of your color that the police officers in our predominantly white neighborhood stop you to "talk" when you walk our dog. You think they're being friendly, but when you tell me that one of their first questions is always, "Do you live around here?" I know that they question your right to be here, that somehow your being here threatens their sense of security....

I did not have to be told much when I was your age. When I was growing up in Louisiana in the 1950s and 1960s, the color lines were very clearly drawn. I followed my mother to the back entrance of the doctor's office, marked "colored." I knew which water fountain I was supposed to drink from. On the bus ride to my all-black school, I watched white children walk to schools just two or three blocks from my house.

In large part, my childhood years were wrapped in the warm cocoon of family and community who all knew each other and looked out for one another. However, I remember clearly my racing heart, my sweaty-palmed fear of the white policemen who entered my father's small restaurant one night and hit him with nightsticks, the helpless terror when there were rumors in our school yard that the Ku Klux Klan would be riding, the anxiety of knowing my college-aged foster sister had joined the civil-rights marchers in a face-off against the white policemen and their dogs. And, I remember, my Maya, the death of your grandfather when I was seven, who died of kidney failure because the "colored" ward wasn't yet allowed the use of the brand-new dialysis machine.

Your world is very different, at least on its surface. In many ways now is a more confusing time to live....

As any mother would, I have a great need to protect you, but it is hard to know how. My childhood experience was different from yours....

CONTINUED

**Reproducible 2.1**
**Page 2 of 2**

When I was in my segregated, all-black elementary school, we were told by teachers and parents that we had to excel, that we had to "do better than" any white kids because the world was already on their side. When your cousin Joey was in high school, I remember berating him for getting a "D" in chemistry. His response was, "What do you expect of me? The white kids get C's." Recently a colleague tried to help an African-American middle-schooler to learn multiplication. The student looked up at the teacher and said, "Why are you trying to teach me this? Black people don't multiply. Multiplication is for white people." You know, Maya, I think that may be the biggest challenge you and other brown children will face — not believing the limits that others place upon you.*

1.    What adjectives does Delpit use to describe the lessons of segregation? What are the lessons she wants her daughter to learn from her experience? How have her experiences as a young girl shaped her attitudes today?

2.    What would you like Lisa Delpit and her daughter to know about your experiences with race and racism? How have those experiences shaped your identity?

3.    Why do you think Lisa Delpit believes that "in many ways now is a more confusing time to live"? In what sense is it more confusing? In her view, how does that confusion shape the way young African Americans view their identity? Do you agree with her assessment?

_____

* Lisa Delpit, "Explaining Racism." *Harvard Graduate School of Education,* Spring 2000, pp. 15–17.

**Reproducible 2.2**
**Page 1 of 2**

## "That Was the Way It Was Supposed to Be"

Segregation shaped the attitudes and values of both white and African Americans. Like Lisa Delpit, Daniel Dyer is an educator who grew up in the 1950s and 1960s. He writes:

I was nearly 20 years old before I spoke to a black person.

In 1944, I was born in Enid, Oklahoma.... In my boyhood I never questioned segregation, it was merely a fact of my existence....

At the time, I saw nothing immoral, or even extraordinary, about the divided city I lived in. If the backs of the city buses bore painted signs that said COLORED ONLY; if the department stores featured separate drinking fountains and restrooms (WHITE and COLORED); if black citizens of Enid swam in different pools, played in different parks, attended different churches and schools (whites went to Enid High School, blacks to Booker T. Washington); well, that was the way it was supposed to be. That's all....

My racial beliefs were confirmed by everything I read, saw, and heard. Comic books contained racial stereotypes; movies and cartoons featured black characters who were superstitious, cowardly, dirty, ignorant, and incapable of speaking "real" English....

My father joined the faculty of Hiram College in 1956, and I entered the seventh grade at the Hiram [Ohio] Local Schools. Racially, things were not all that different from Enid. There were no black students in the school system, not during the entire six years I attended it.

But for the first time in my life, I did participate in an activity with blacks: highschool basketball.... Although I recall no racial incidents at those games, I do remember being frightened before tip-off. I was playing, you see, against aliens.

Racist jokes and behavior were normal during my high school years.... As a sophomore, I performed in blackface in the school play, enacting crude racial caricatures to the great amusement of the all-white audience.

And it is with great embarrassment that I remember driving with my equally brainless buddies through a black neighborhood in Ravenna, car windows down, yelling vile insults at black pedestrians. Those moments are the most unforgivable of my life.

CONTINUED

**Reproducible 2.2**
**Page 2 of 2**

> My years as a student at Hiram College ... changed my life. For the first time, I was attending classes with blacks, eating with them, living with them. There were not many, mind you, but their excellence in virtually every area of college life began quietly to invade the roots of my racism; before long, the entire tree was sick. And dying....
>
> I cannot claim to be free of all racism; after all, there is something unpleasantly permanent about many experiences and lessons of our childhood.*

1.  Dyer describes two communities he lived in as a child. How did each determine who belonged and who did not? How did those definitions shape and misshape the way he viewed the world?

2.  Dyer describes the racism that marked his high school years. Why do you think he participated? What does he suggest about the links between the racial stereotypes he encountered in books and movies and his own behavior?

3.  Dyer recalls a machine called a fluoroscope that was widely used in shoe stores in the 1950s. Shoppers would stick their feet inside the machine to see how well their shoes fit. Dyer writes, "I remember ... sticking my feet repeatedly into that machine. I was fascinated by the X-ray image of the bones of my feet.... The countless doses of radiation that machine so innocently gave me ... will always be with me and may even have permanently damaged me, even though shoe-store fluoroscopes are now as illegal as ... segregation." What point is he trying to make about the legacies of segregation?

---

* Daniel Dyer, "Racial Background Is Not a Halo But an Accident" *The Cleveland Plain Dealer,* January, 7, 1993. Reprinted by permission.

# LESSON 2: The Legal Basis for Segregation: Plessy v. Ferguson

**Central Question:** What are the consequences of dividing people by race?

## Getting Started

How did segregation begin? Was it a law or a custom? How is segregation linked to race and racism? Explain to students that over the next few days, they will be exploring the history of segregation and the ways it affected American life.

## Background Information

In 1865, in the final days of the Civil War, Congress approved an amendment abolishing slavery in the United States. Once the war ended, each Confederate state had to approve the 13th Amendment before it could return to its place in the Union. The newly readmitted states were willing to abolish slavery but were not willing to accept African Americans as equals. State after state in the former Confederacy passed the so-called Black Codes, laws that tried to limit the freedom of former slaves. The codes spelled out what work African Americans would be allowed to do. They also placed limits on the rights of African Americans.

Congress responded to the Black Codes with a series of laws jointly known as Reconstruction. These laws placed the former Confederate states under military rule and set requirements for readmission to the Union, including approval not only of the 13th Amendment, but also the 14th and 15th amendments. The 14th Amendment granted U.S. citizenship to all former slaves and declared that all citizens had the same rights and privileges. The amendment passed Congress on June 13, 1866, and was ratified on July 9, 1868. The 15th Amendment ensured that a citizen's race, color, or prior history as a slave could not be used to keep that individual from voting. Congress passed the amendment on February 26, 1869, and it was ratified on February 3, 1870.

Despite the three amendments, the rights of African Americans were under attack almost everywhere in the nation in the late nineteenth century. For example, in 1883, the Supreme Court ruled that the Civil Rights Act of 1875, which outlawed discrimination, was unconstitutional because it violated the right of businesses, institutions, and civic organizations to choose customers, employees, and/or members. The justices claimed that the 14th Amendment applied only to state governments.

A few years later, an African American from Louisiana named Homer Plessy challenged segregation on streetcars. He claimed that segregation violated his rights as a citizen of the United States. In 1896, in the case of *Plessy v. Ferguson*, the U.S. Supreme Court ruled against Plessy. Eight of the nine justices argued that separate facilities for African Americans do not violate their rights as long as those facilities are equal to those provided for white Americans. Only one justice disagreed. In his dissent, John Marshall Harlan, a former slave-holder from Kentucky, wrote: "In respect of civil rights, all citizens are equal before the law. The humblest is the peer [equal] of the most powerful. The law regards man as man, and takes no account of his surroundings or of his color when his civil rights as guaranteed by the supreme law of the land are involved." Nearly 60 years would pass before the Supreme Court heeded Harlan's words.

## Activity: Summarizing the Main Idea

When the Civil War ended, three amendments were added to the U.S. Constitution. Review how an amendment is added to the Constitution. A proposed amendment is sent to the states for approval if it has been passed by a two-thirds vote in both the House of Representatives and the Senate. To be added to the Constitution, it needs state approval. It is considered approved when passed by three-quarters of the states. Since its adoption in 1789, the U.S. Constitution has been amended or changed only 27 times and 10 of those amendments (the Bill of Rights) were added almost immediately after the Constitution was ratified. Not surprisingly, when an amendment is ratified, it is front-page news. Distribute **Reproducible 2.3** and explain that it contains the three amendments added after the Civil War. Have students read each amendment with a partner and then write a headline announcing its ratification.

Explain that a good headline summarizes the main idea of an event in 12 words or less. You may want to use the 13th Amendment to model the process. Ask students to read the amendment and explain its purpose (end slavery). Discuss why the ratification of the 13th Amendment was a major news story. (Disagreements over slavery were a major cause of the Civil War; slavery had been in existence in what is now the United States for over 250 years.) Headlines might read: "Free at Last! 13th Amendment Outlaws Slavery" or "No More Slavery; 13th Amendment Is the Law of the Land."

## Activity: Interpreting the Constitution

Explain to students that the three amendments did not end discrimination against African Americans. As soon as Reconstruction ended, many Southern states passed laws requiring separation of the races. In 1896, a man named Homer Plessy challenged those laws in a case that eventually reached the U.S. Supreme Court. Distribute **Reproducible 2.4** and ask students to read the facts of the case and decide how they think the 14th Amendment applies to the case. After students have shared their opinions, distribute **Reproducible 2.5**. It explains how the Supreme Court actually decided the case.

Have students read both the majority view and the dissenting opinion. Explain that justices who do not agree with the majority have the right to issue a separate opinion. In this case, Justice John Marshall Harlan disagreed with the majority and wrote his own opinion. Ask students how they think the majority decision will affect everyday life in the United States.

### Homework Activity: Expressing an Opinion

As a homework assignment, ask students to imagine that they and their families lived in the 1890s. Have them write a letter to a family member describing what they think the impact of the Supreme Court decision in *Plessy v. Ferguson* will have on their family and the nation.

### Writing Suggestions

- What does "created equal" mean to you? Does it mean equal treatment under the law, equal opportunities, or equal education?
- Can "separate but equal" be equal?
- What does Justice Harlan mean when he says the Constitution is color-blind? Do you agree? Should the Constitution be color-blind?

Reproducible 2.3
Page 1 of 2

# The 13th, 14th, and 15th Amendments

Read each amendment and decide what its purpose is. (You may want to consult the glossary of legal terms on page 2.) Then write a headline announcing the ratification of the amendment. Remember that headlines summarize the main idea of a story in 12 words or less.

## Amendment XIII (Ratified December 6, 1865)

1.  Neither slavery nor involuntary servitude, except as a punishment for crime whereof the party shall have been duly convicted, shall exist within the United States, or any place subject to their jurisdiction.

2.  Congress shall have power to enforce this article by appropriate legislation.

**The headline reads ...**

## Amendment XIV (Ratified July 9, 1868)

1.  All persons born or naturalized in the United States, and subject to the jurisdiction thereof, are citizens of the United States and of the State wherein they reside. No State shall make or enforce any law which shall abridge the privileges or immunities of citizens of the United States; nor shall any State deprive any person of life, liberty, or property, without due process of law; nor deny to any person within its jurisdiction the equal protection of the laws....

5.  The Congress shall have power to enforce, by appropriate legislation, the provisions of this article.

**The headline reads ...**

CONTINUED

**Reproducible 2.3**
**Page 2 of 2**

### Amendment XV (Ratified February 3, 1870)

1.      The right of citizens of the United States to vote shall not be denied or abridged by the United States or by any State on account of race, color, or previous condition of servitude.

2.      The Congress shall have power to enforce this article by appropriate legislation.

**The headline reads ...**

### Glossary

| | |
|---|---|
| **abridge** | reduce |
| **amend** | change or add to |
| **amendment** | a change in a constitution or other legal document |
| **deprive** | take away |
| **due process** | the legal protections a citizen has when a state, nation, or court makes a decision that could affect their rights. The most basic rights protected under due process is the right to know what crimes an individual has been charged with and the right to have one's own version of the story heard in court. |
| **immunity** | a release from or an exception to a law. For example, a court may decide that the testimony of a witness in one case will not be used against the witness at their own trial. The witness receives *immunity*. |
| **jurisdiction** | the right of a court to make decisions that must be obeyed in a particular geographic area — a city, state, or, in the case of the U.S. Supreme Court, the nation |
| **naturalize** | to give citizenship to someone born in another country |

**Reproducible 2.4**

# The Dispute in *Plessy v. Ferguson*

Homer Plessy was a citizen of the United States and a resident of the state of Louisiana. On June 7, 1892, he purchased a first-class ticket on the East Louisiana Railway from New Orleans to Covington, Louisiana. He entered a passenger car and took an empty seat in a car reserved for the whites only. The conductor demanded that he leave his seat and move to a car reserved for the "colored race." When Plessy refused to move, he was arrested. He was brought to trial and found guilty of violating a state law requiring segregation on trains. Plessy appealed the decision of John Ferguson, the judge who claimed that as long as the railroad offered "separate but equal" seating, Plessy's rights were protected. Plessy disagreed. He argued that the law was unconstitutional — that is, it went against the 14th Amendment.

How the case is decided depends upon whether a law passed by the state of Louisiana in 1890 requiring separate railroad cars for Black and white passengers is in keeping with the U.S. Constitution. The first section of the law states:

> All railway companies carrying passengers in their coaches in this state, shall provide separate but equal accommodations for the white and colored races.... No person or persons shall be permitted to occupy seats in coaches, other than the ones assigned to them, on account of the race they belong to.

1.  Reread the 14th Amendment (Reproducible 2.4.) Does the amendment allow states to pass segregation laws?


2.  Discuss the case with your partner. Then briefly describe what you decided.

**Reproducible 2.5**

# What the Court Decided

**Mr. Justice Henry B. BROWN delivered the majority opinion of the Supreme Court on May 18, 1896.** He wrote in part:

> The object of the [14th] Amendment was undoubtedly to enforce the absolute equality of the two races before the law, but in the nature of things, it could not have been intended to abolish distinctions based upon color, or to enforce social, as distinguished from political equality, or commingling [mixing] of the two races upon terms unsatisfactory to either. Laws permitting, and even requiring their separation, in places where they are liable to be brought into contact, do not necessarrily imply the inferiority of either race to the other, and have been generally, if not universally, recognized as within the competency [responsibilities] of the state legislatures in the exercise of their police power.
>
> … If one race be inferior to the other civilly or politically, the Constitution of the United States cannot put them on the same plane.

**Mr. Justice John Marshall HARLAN dissented.** He wrote in part:

> It is said in argument that the statute of Louisiana does not discriminate again either race, but prescribes a rule applicable alike to white and colored citizens. But… every one knows that the statute in question had its origin in the purpose, not so much to exclude white persons from railroad cars occupied by blacks, as to exclude colored people from coaches occupied by or assigned to white persons…. Further, if this statute of Louisiana is consistent with the personal liberty of citizens, why may not the state require the separation in railroad coaches of native and naturalized citizens of the United States, or of Protestants and Roman Catholics? …
>
> The white race deems itself to be the dominant race in this country. And so it is, in prestige, in achievements, in education, in wealth, and in power…. But in view of the constitution, in the eye of the law, there is in this country no superior, dominant, ruling class of citizens…. Our constitution is color-blind, and neither knows nor tolerates classes among citizens. In respect of civil rights, all citizens are equal before the law.

Imagine that you were alive in 1896 and read about the Supreme Court's decision in the case of *Plessy v. Ferguson* in your local newspaper. Write a letter to a family member describing the impact you think the decision will have on your family and the nation.

# LESSON 3: The Consequences of *Plessy v. Ferguson*

**Central Question:** What are the consequences of dividing people by race?

## Getting Started

Ask volunteers to share their predictions about the effects of the court's decision in the case of *Plessy v. Ferguson* (Homework, Lesson 2). Then show students Section 2 of *The Road to Brown*, "Plessy & the Era of Jim Crow." (Preview the section so that you can stop the video, if you wish to do so, before the very graphic lynching scenes at the end of the section.) Remind students of their earlier definitions of segregation. Encourage them to add to or even revise those definitions.

## Background Information

The Supreme Court decision in the case of *Plessy v. Ferguson* (1896) permitted the growth of a system of state and local laws known as "Jim Crow" laws. They established racial barriers in almost every aspect of American life. In many places, Black and white Americans could not publicly sit, drink, or eat side by side. Churches, theaters, parks, even cemeteries were segregated. "By the early 1900s," writes historian Lerone Bennett, Jr., "America was two nations — one white, one black, separate and unequal." He likens segregation to "a wall, a system, a way of separating people from people." That wall did not go up in a single day; it was built "brick by brick, bill by bill, fear by fear."

## Activity: Analyzing Primary Sources

Divide the class into six small groups and give each group one of three packets. Each packet provides evidence of the effects that *Plessy v. Ferguson* had on American life. The two "A" groups will examine photographs showing evidence of segregation. The "B" groups will analyze segregation laws. The "C" groups will study graphs and tables created by a U.S. government commission in 1946 to show the consequences of segregation.

After giving students time to examine their packet, ask them to identify at least three things they learned about segregation from the evidence it provides. Allow groups about 15 minutes to prepare their lists. Then redivide the class into groups of three. (Each group should contain at least one member from each the A, B, and C groups.) Have each member share their packet and explain what they learned from it about segregation. Then ask the groups to use the combined lists to write two sentences — the first should define segregation, and the second should describe its impact on American life.

## Writing Suggestions

- What did you learn about segregation from this lesson?
  What surprised you about the evidence you examined?
- What does the evidence suggest about whether "separate but equal" can ever be equal?
- Some people believe that segregation was not about race but about power.
  To what extent does the evidence support that idea?

## State and Local Segregations Laws

Segregations laws touched every aspect of everyday life. For example, in 1935, Oklahoma prohibited African Americans and whites from boating together. In 1905, Georgia established separate parks for Black and white people. In 1930, Birmingham, Alabama, made it illegal for the two races to play checkers or dominoes together. The Martin Luther King, Jr., National Historic Site Interpretive Staff compiled the following list:

- *Barbers.* No colored barber shall serve as a barber (to) white girls or women (Georgia).

- *Blind Wards.* The board of trustees shall ... maintain a separate building ... on separate ground for the admission, care, instruction, and support of all blind persons of the colored or Black race (Louisiana).

- *Burial.* The officer in charge shall not bury, or allow to be buried, any colored persons upon ground set apart or used for the burial of white persons (Georgia).

- *Buses.* All passenger stations in this state operated by any motor transportation company shall have separate waiting rooms or space and separate ticket windows for the white and colored races (Alabama).

- *Child Custody.* It shall be unlawful for any parent, relative, or other white person in this State, having the control or custody of any white child, by right of guardianship, natural or acquired, or otherwise, to dispose of, give or surrender such white child permanently into the custody, control, maintenance, or support, of a Negro (South Carolina).

- *Education.* The schools for white children and the schools for Negro children shall be conducted separately (Florida).

- *Libraries.* The state librarian is directed to fit up and maintain a separate place for the use of the colored people who may come to the library for the purpose of reading books or periodicals (North Carolina).

- *Mental Hospitals.* The Board of Control shall see that proper and distinct apartments are arranged for said patients, so that in no case shall Negroes and white persons be together (Georgia).

CONTINUED

- *Militia.* The white and colored militia shall be separately enrolled, and shall never be compelled to serve in the same organization. No organization of colored troops shall be permitted where white troops are available, and colored troops shall be under the command of white officers (North Carolina).

- *Nurses.* No person or corporation shall require any white female nurse to nurse in wards or rooms in hospitals, either public or private, in which Negro men are placed (Alabama).

- *Prisons.* The warden shall see that the white convicts shall have separate apartments for both eating and sleeping from the Negro convicts (Mississippi).

- *Reform Schools.* The children of white and colored races committed to the houses of reform shall be kept entirely separate from each other (Kentucky).

- *Teaching.* Any instructor who shall teach in any school, college, or institution where members of the white and colored race are received and enrolled as pupils for instruction shall be deemed guilty of a misdemeanor, and upon conviction thereof, shall be fined ... (Oklahoma).

- *Wine and Beer.* All persons licensed to conduct the business of selling beer or wine ... shall serve either white people exclusively or colored people exclusively and shall not sell to the two races within the same room at any time (Georgia).

**In addition:**
- Racially separate washrooms required in factories and mines (6 states)
- White and Black prisoners could not be chained together (6 states)
- Segregated parks, playgrounds, bathing and fishing and boating facilities, amusement parks, racetracks, pool halls, circuses, theaters, and public halls (8 states)
- Separate waiting rooms for bus and train travelers (10 states)
- African Americans required to sit in the backs of buses and streetcars (11 states)
- Segregated railroad passengers on trips within the state's borders (14 states)
- Segregated mental patients (14 states)
- Segregated public schools (14 states with 11.5 million students and 4 other states allowed segregation if local communities wanted it)*

---

* This list was derived from a larger list composed by the Martin Luther King, Jr., National Historic Site Interpretive Staff. Last Updated January 5, 1998. http//www.nps.gov/malu/documents/jim crowlaws.htm.

## School Segregation: May 18, 1954

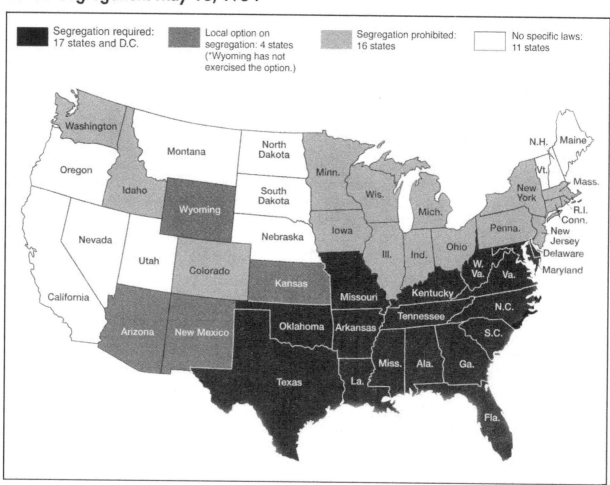

| | Segregation required: 17 states and D.C. | | Local option on segregation: 4 states (*Wyoming has not exercised the option.) | | Segregation prohibited: 16 states | | No specific laws: 11 states |

Reprinted from Sanford Wexler, *The Civil Rights Movement: An Eyewitness History.* Facts on File, 1993.

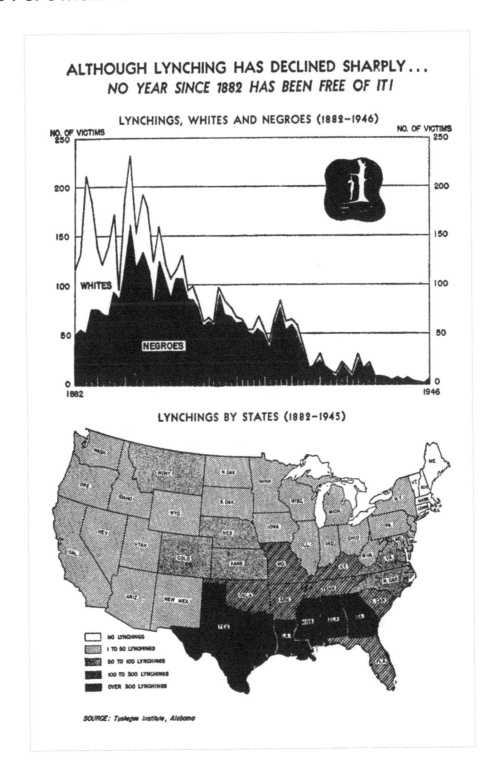

Reprinted from *To Secure These Rights: Report of the President's Committee on Civil Rights*, 1946.

| State or District of Columbia | Average annual salary of principals, supervisors, and teachers in schools for— | |
| --- | --- | --- |
| | Whites | Negroes |
| Alabama................................ | $1,158 | $661 |
| Arkansas................................ | 924 | 555 |
| Delaware................................ | 1,953 | 1,814 |
| Florida................................ | 1,530 | 970 |
| Georgia................................ | 1,123 | 515 |
| Louisiana................................ | 1,683 | 828 |
| Maryland................................ | 2,085 | 2,002 |
| Mississippi................................ | 1,107 | 342 |
| Missouri................................ | 1,397 | 1,590 [1] |
| North Carolina........................ | 1,380 | 1,249 |
| Oklahoma................................ | 1,428 | 1,438 |
| South Carolina........................ | 1,203 | 615 |
| Tennessee................................ | 1,071 | 1,010 |
| Texas................................ | 1,395 | 946 |
| Virginia................................ | 1,364 | 1,129 |
| District of Columbia.................... | 2,610 | 2,610 |

[1] Higher salaries due to the fact that most Negro schools are located in cities where all salaries are higher.

Reprinted from *To Secure These Rights: Report of the President's Committee on Civil Rights*, 1946.

# THE NATION'S CAPITAL
## A SYMBOL OF FREEDOM AND EQUALITY?

IF HE DECIDES TO REMAIN IN D. C. OVERNIGHT HE WILL FIND THAT:

HE CANNOT EAT IN A DOWNTOWN RESTAURANT

HE CANNOT ATTEND A DOWNTOWN MOVIE OR PLAY.

HE CANNOT SLEEP IN A DOWNTOWN HOTEL.

IF HE DECIDES TO STAY IN D. C.

➤ HE USUALLY MUST FIND A HOME IN AN OVERCROWDED, SUB-STANDARD, SEGREGATED AREA:

NEGRO-OCCUPIED DWELLINGS
40% SUBSTANDARD

WHITE-OCCUPIED DWELLINGS
12% SUBSTANDARD

➤ HE MUST SEND HIS CHILDREN TO INFERIOR JIM CROW SCHOOLS:

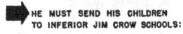

WHITES — CAPACITY EXCEEDS ENROLLMENT BY 27%

NEGROES — ENROLLMENT EXCEEDS CAPACITY BY 8%

➤ HE MUST ENTRUST HIS FAMILY'S HEALTH TO MEDICAL AGENCIES WHICH GIVE THEM INFERIOR SERVICES:

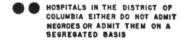

●● HOSPITALS IN THE DISTRICT OF COLUMBIA EITHER DO NOT ADMIT NEGROES OR ADMIT THEM ON A SEGREGATED BASIS

Reprinted from *To Secure These Rights: Report of the President's Committee on Civil Rights*, 1946.

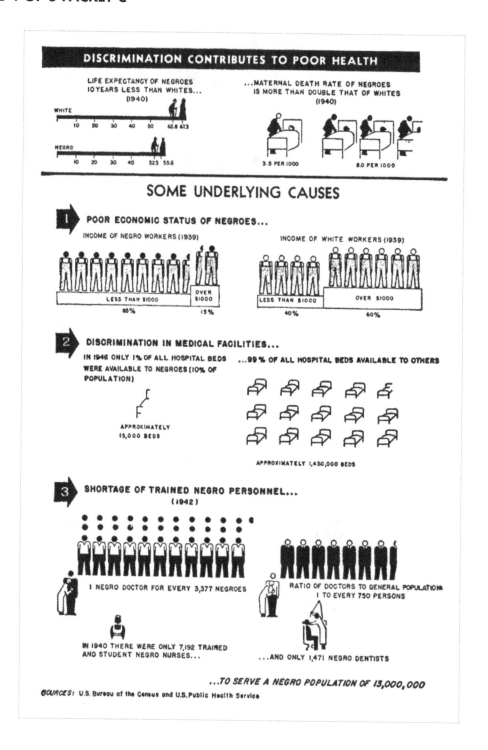

Reprinted from *To Secure These Rights: Report of the President's Committee on Civil Rights,* 1946.

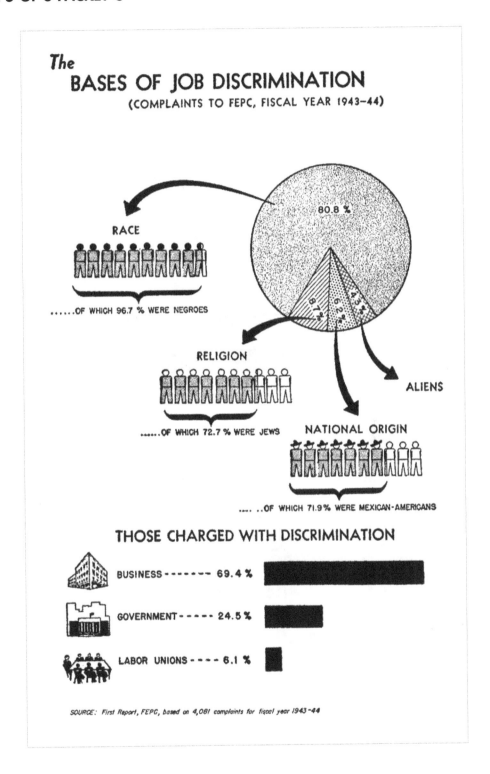

Reprinted from *To Secure These Rights: Report of the President's Committee on Civil Rights,* 1946.

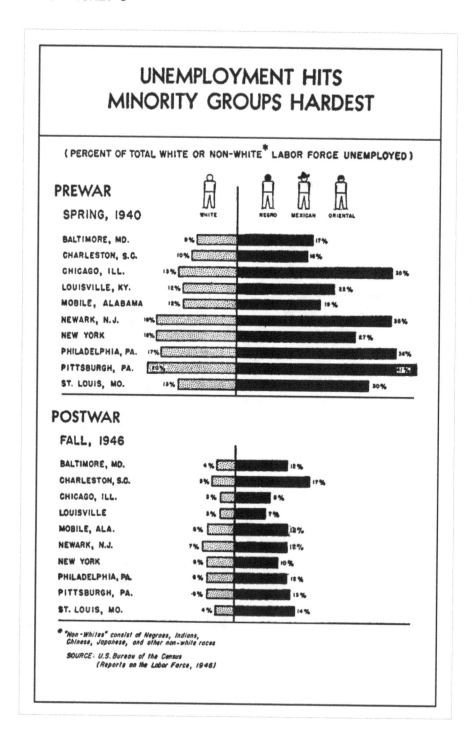

Reprinted from *To Secure These Rights: Report of the President's Committee on Civil Rights*, 1946.

# LESSON 4: The Road to *Brown v. Board of Education*

**Central Question:** How can individuals and groups in a democracy organize to correct injustices?

## Getting Started

Ask students to imagine what it must have been like to live in a segregated society. How might African Americans express their outrage? How might they persuade other Americans to join them in destroying the system? Record students' ideas on the board and return to them as the lesson progresses.

## Background Information

In the late 1800s and early 1900s, Americans formed a number of organizations to express their outrage at segregation and attack the laws that supported it. Among them was the National Association for the Advancement of Colored People (NAACP). Its founders included both Black and white Americans. In 1935, the group decided to systematically challenge segregation in the nation's courts. Professor Charles Houston of Howard University Law School led a special legal team with the help of Thurgood Marshall, a former student of Houston's. After Houston retired, Marshall took charge of the team. The aim was to attack segregation by challenging the idea central to *Plessy v. Ferguson* — the idea that separate facilities are truly equal. The team's first cases dealt with segregation in higher education. Few states could afford to provide "separate but equal" legal, medical, and other professional training for Black and white students.

Slowly, the legal team assembled by Houston and Marshall made progress. In 1949, the Supreme Court ruled that a Texas law school set up only for African American students was not equal to the state's all-white law school [*Sweatt v. Painter*]. In a 1950 decision [*McLaurin v. Oklahoma*], the justices concluded that an African American student who was allowed to enroll at the University of Oklahoma's law school was not receiving an education equal to that of white students as long as he was kept apart from his classmates in the classroom, cafeteria, and library. The court ruled that "such restrictions impair and inhibit his ability to study, engage in discussions and exchange views with other students, and in general, to learn his profession."

Little by little, ruling by ruling, the NAACP was tearing down the legal wall that separated Americans. After chipping away at segregation in higher education, NAACP lawyers turned their attention to segregation in the nation's public schools. This time they would argue that even if separate facilities were equal, they would still violate the 14th Amendment. The lawyers filed law suits in four states and the District of Columbia. Each challenged the constitutionality of separating children by race. In late 1952, the justices decided that the cases were so similar that they should be heard together. So they combined them into a single case that came to be known as *Brown et al. v. Board of Education of Topeka et al.* The Supreme Court's decision came in May 1954. It declared that racial segregation in public schools was unconstitutional.

When the Supreme Court issued its decision in the *Brown* case, the justices did not provide guidelines for complying with the decision. They waited until May 31, 1955, to rule that federal courts were to decide whether a school district was acting in "good faith" by desegregating its schools "with all deliberate speed."

### Activity: Tracing the Effects of a Strategy

Explain that a group of lawyers for the NAACP used the courts to challenge *Plessy v. Ferguson*. The group understood that overturning the decision would take time. They would have to build precedents — that is, they would have to create a new understanding of the law through a series of judicial decisions. A *precedent* is a judicial decision in an earlier case with facts and law similar to a dispute currently before a court.

Show about 15 minutes of the video, *The Second American Revolution* (from the conversation between Ruby Dee and Ossie Davis at the Howard University Law Library through the acceptance of the Clarks' psychological evidence by the Supreme Court). Ask students to notice how one court decision builds a precedent for the next. Ask students to work alone or with a partner to create a cartoon or other drawing that explains the strategy of the NAACP.

### Activity: Analyzing a Supreme Court Decision

Ask students to read the summary of the *Brown* decision on **Reproducible 2.6**. Have them underline words and phrases that suggest the justices based their case on precedent — a decision in an earlier case with facts and law similar to a dispute currently before a court — and on the psychological evidence Kenneth Clark's experiments provided. Have students decide what they think the next step will be in the struggle to overturn segregation.

### Activity: Expressing an Opinion

Distribute **Reproducible 2.7** and explain to students that the cartoon expresses the artist's opinion of efforts to enforce the Brown decision and end segregation. Have students work with a partner to answer the questions that accompany the cartoon. Then ask students to write a paragraph or create a cartoon or drawing that expresses their view of the impact the *Brown* decision is likely to have on students across the nation. Be sure that students include a title for their cartoon. The cartoons should show an understanding of *segregation* and its impact on American life and recognize that enforcement of the *Brown* decision will alter the way Americans live and work.

**Writing Suggestions**

- Why were the dolls important in the case of *Brown v. Board of Education*? What did the Clarks learn from them about the effects of segregation on African American children? What did they reveal to the justices on the Supreme Court?

- How did the justices in the *Brown* case interpret the 14th Amendment? How did their interpretation differ from the way the justices in *Plessy v. Ferguson* viewed the amendment?

- Why do you think the NAACP chose to use the courts to attack segregation? What other methods might they have used? What were the advantages and disadvantages of each?

- How might you or someone you know try to right a wrong or stop an injustice? What methods would you choose? What allies would you seek?

**Reproducible 2.6**

347 U.S. 483
Argued December 9, 1952
Reargued December 8, 1953
Decided May 17, 1954

**APPEAL FROM THE UNITED STATES DISTRICT COURT
FOR THE DISTRICT OF KANSAS**

Segregation of white and Negro children in the public schools of a State solely on the basis of race, pursuant to state laws permitting or requiring such segregation, denies to Negro children the equal protection of the laws guaranteed by the Fourteenth Amendment — even though the physical facilities and other "tangible" factors of white and Negro schools may be equal.

(a) The history of the Fourteenth Amendment is inconclusive as to its intended effect on public education.

(b) The question presented in these cases must be determined not on the basis of conditions existing when the Fourteenth Amendment was adopted, but in the light of the full development of public education and its present place in American life throughout the Nation.

(c) Where a State has undertaken to provide an opportunity for an education in its public schools, such an opportunity is a right, which must be made available to all on equal terms.

(d) Segregation of children in public schools solely on the basis of race deprives children of the minority group of equal educational opportunities, even though the physical facilities and other "tangible" factors may be equal.

(e) The "separate but equal" doctrine adopted in *Plessy v. Ferguson*, 163 U.S. 537, has no place in the field of public education.

<u>Glossary</u>

inconclusive    questionable; open to doubt

pursuant of    in agreement with

tangible    real; capable of being touched or felt

**Reproducible 2.7**

## "Inch by Inch"

1. Describe exactly what you see in the cartoon. Pay attention to shapes and the position of people and/or objects. Notice the scale used in the drawing.

2. What symbol does the cartoonist use to show school segregation?
   What do the children in the drawing stand for?

3. What is the message of the cartoon?

4. Bill Mauldin called his cartoon "Inch by Inch." What other title might be appropriate?

# PART 3: Choices in Little Rock

# PART 3: Choices in Little Rock

## Central Question

- How do the choices people make, individually and collectively, shape a society?

## Student Outcomes

- Explores the choices of individuals and groups during the crisis in Little Rock in 1957
- Understands the challenges of federalism
- Analyzes the ways individuals and groups use the Constitution to protect their rights
- Uses primary sources to identify point of view, attitude, and intent
- Compares and contrasts various decisions and their consequences
- Uses logic and reason to defend a point of view

## Teaching Focus

Part 3 examines the decisions people made in Little Rock, Arkansas, in 1957 in response to *Brown v. Board of Education*. Those decisions had short-term and long-term consequences.

# LESSON 1: The First Day of School

**Central Question:** How do the choices people make, individually and collectively, shape a society?

### Getting Started

Part 3 examines the decisions people in Little Rock, Arkansas, made in response to *Brown v. Board of Education*. Lesson 1 begins in September 1957 with the desegregation of the city's largest and most prestigious high school — Central High. You may wish to use **Reproducible 3.1** to introduce the nine African American students who were chosen to integrate the school.

Ask students to recall their first day at a new school. What did they expect the day to be like? What did they fear? What did they look forward to? How did they prepare for the day? What surprised them about the experience? Tell students that they are going to learn what the first day of school was like for the first African American students to attend Central High.

### Background Information

In 1955, Virgil Blossom, the superintendent of schools in Little Rock, announced a plan to integrate the schools gradually beginning in 1957 with Central High, one of three high schools in the city. The other two were Horace Mann, a high school for African American students, and Hall, a new all-white school located in a well-to-do section of the city. Neither Horace Mann nor Hall was scheduled for immediate integration.

As required by law, the school board sent Blossom's plan to a federal district court for approval. Despite challenges from African Americans who wanted to speed up the process and white Americans who wanted to stop it, the court approved the plan, and by the summer of 1957, school officials had selected 17 African American students from over 200 applicants for enrollment at Central High.

School officials rejected many of the applicants because their grades were not high enough. Others were rejected because officials did not think they could handle the pressures of being a small minority in a school that was overwhelmingly white. (The plan called for the enrollment of fewer than 17 African American students in a school attended by about 2,000 white students.) Still other African American students dropped out on their own after the superintendent told them that they would not be allowed to participate in sports or any other extracurricular activity. As resistance to integration became more vocal in the summer of 1957 in Little Rock and elsewhere, a number of parents withdrew their children out of fear for their safety.

By the time school opened, only nine African American students were prepared to attend Central High School — Minnijean Brown, Elizabeth Eckford, Ernest Green, Thelma Mothershed, Melba Pattillo, Gloria Ray, Terrence Roberts, Jefferson Thomas, and Carlotta Walls. Despite the talk on TV and the radio and in the newspapers, the "Little Rock Nine" did not believe that integration would lead to violence in Little Rock. Ernest Green recalls:

> There hadn't been any trouble expected, given the fact that there had been other schools in Arkansas that had been integrated — Fort Smith, Arkansas, and some others. The buses in Little Rock had been desegregated without any problem. The library was integrated; the medical school and the law school at the University had admitted some blacks. So there was an expectation that there would be minimal problems, but nothing major that would put Little Rock on the map. The first indication that I had of it was the night before we were to go to school, the Labor Day Monday night. [Governor] Orval Faubus came on TV and indicated that he was calling out the [Arkansas] National Guard to prevent our entrance into Central because of what he thought were threats to our lives. He was doing it for our own "protection." Even at that time that was his line. He said that the troops would be out in front of the school and they would bar our entrance to Central — for our protection as well as for the protection and tranquility of the city.[7]

After hearing Governor Faubus on television, Blossom asked the "Little Rock Nine" to stay home Tuesday morning, while he sought guidance from U.S. District Judge Ronald N. Davies. The judge ordered the school board to proceed with integration as planned. The "Little Rock Nine" were to report to Central High the next day — Wednesday, September 4. Fearful for their safety, Daisy Bates, the president of the Arkansas NAACP, suggested that they come to school as a group. She planned to ask religious leaders in the city to accompany them.

Fifteen-year-old Elizabeth Eckford knew nothing of the plan. In her haste, Daisy Bates had forgotten to get word to her. So early Wednesday morning, Eckford ironed the dress she made for her first day at Central High, said good-bye to her worried parents, and set off for school, alone.

When Eckford reached Central High, she found herself surrounded by an angry crowd that taunted and threatened her as she tried to enter the building. The soldiers who guarded the building turned her away. Unsure of what to do and terrified of the mob, Eckford quickly headed for a bus stop even as the crowd continued to scream and jeer.

---

[7] Henry Hampton and Steve Fayer, *Voices of Freedom: An Oral History of the Civil Rights Movement from the 1950s through the 1980s.* Vintage, 1990, p.39.

**Activity: Interpreting Points of View**

Ask students to read Elizabeth Eckford's account of her arrival at Central High School on **Reproducible 3.2**. If you wish to have students listen to her account as they read, go to www.facinghistory.org. A recording entitled "In Her Own Words" can be found under "Crisis in Little Rock, Arkansas," which is part of the Choosing to Participate Exhibition. Ask students to focus on the choices Eckford made that morning. Why didn't she turn on the crowd that followed her to the bus stop? What might have happened had she done so?

Next focus students' attention on the photographs on pages 2 and 3 of **Reproducible 3.2**. Ask students to record what they see in each photograph without trying to interpret the image. Then have students work with a partner to decide what the photographer is trying to say. After discussing their interpretation, have each pair write a caption or a title for the two photos. Ask partners to share their captions with the class. What do the captions have in common? How do students account for differences in the way the class interpreted the images?

Point out that not everyone in the two photographs was harassing Eckford. Some people were *bystanders* — people who witness an event but are neither victims nor perpetrators. (Remind students that the word *perpetrator* means wrongdoer — in this case, a person who called Eckford names and threatened her life.) Marcia Webb, a white student at Central High and a bystander on September 4, 1957, later reflected on her choices that morning:

> I remember the picture in the newspaper of Elizabeth Eckford with the jeering white faces behind her. And at that moment I thought, Marcie, you were there and you never once thought about what was going on with Elizabeth Eckford. You were glad there weren't any violent demonstrations; you were glad no one was hurt physically. But then I realized what hurt can come from words, from silence even, from just being ignored. And when I think about it now, I think about it with regret. I'm sorry to say now looking back that what was happening didn't have more significance and I didn't take more of an active role. But I was interested in the things that most kids are.[8]

What is the pain that comes from names and labels, the silence of neighbors or classmates, or "just being ignored"? How might the situation at Central High School have been different if Marcia Webb and other white students had regarded Eckford and other African American students as "kids" much like themselves?

Encourage students to choose an individual who appears in one of the two photos and write a brief story about that person and how they may have come to be at Central High School that morning. Have students share their story with a partner. Which individuals did students choose to write about? What prompted their choices? Marcia Webb regretted the choice she made that day. How do students think the person they chose may have felt about their behavior in years to come?

---

[8]Joan I. Duffy, "A Reunion with History: Central High Will Observe 1957's Rite of Passage." *Memphis Commercial Appeal*, September 21, 1957.

**Discussion Suggestions**

- What is a mob? How is it different from a gathering or a crowd?
- What power do photographs have to change history? Marcia Webb never forgot the image of Elizabeth Eckford that appeared in the newspapers. The same was true for millions of other Americans. Why do you think so many people have described that image as unforgettable?
- In 1987, Elizabeth Eckford said of her ordeal: "I remember this tremendous feeling of being alone and I didn't know how I was going to get out of there. I didn't know whether I would be injured. There was this deafening roar. I could hear individual voices, but I was not conscious of numbers, I was conscious of being alone." What did Eckford mean when she said, "I was conscious of being alone"?
- What turns a group of ordinary people into a mob? What is the power of a mob?
- Perlesta Hollingsworth is an African American who lived near Central High in 1957. In 1997, he told a reporter, "The shocking thing to me in 1957 was the number of whites who didn't participate in the aggression, who wouldn't do anything but look. Neighbors would express dismay, but wouldn't do anything, wouldn't speak out against it, would go ahead and close their doors to it." Many sociologists believe that bystanders influence an event by the amount and the kind of attention they pay to the event. Why do you think many people expressed disappointment or sadness but wouldn't speak out?

**Writing Suggestions**

- Grace Lorch was a bystander who tried to help Elizabeth Eckford by getting her away from the mob. What might have happened if other bystanders had supported Eckford in similar ways? For example, what might have happened if the principal or a group of teachers had opened the doors of the school and escorted the nine students into the building? What might have happened if white students like Marcia Webb had shown support for Elizabeth Eckford? Would Eckford have felt less alone? Would it have altered the outcome that day?
- Have you ever experienced or witnessed an injustice? Write a brief description of what you saw, heard, and felt that day.
- What do you think will happen next in this story?

# The Little Rock Nine

*Top Row, left to right:* Ernest Green, Melba Pattillo, Jefferson Thomas, Carlotta Walls; Daisy Bates (president of the Arkansas NAACP and advisor to the Little Rock Nine), Terrence Roberts.
*Seated, left to right:* Thelma Mothershed, Minnijean Brown, Elizabeth Eckford; Gloria Ray.

**Ernest Green** became the first African American student to graduate from Central High School in 1958. He later earned a bachelor's degree from Michigan State University. Green served as Assistant Secretary of Housing and Urban Affairs in the administration of President Jimmy Carter. He is currently a managing partner and vice president of Lehman Brothers in Washington, D.C.

**Melba Pattillo Beals** is a writer who has worked as a reporter at NBC and *People* magazine. Her memoir, *Warriors Don't Cry*, won several literary awards in 1995. She earned degrees at San Francisco State and Columbia University and today lives in San Francisco.

CONTINUED

**Reproducible 3.1**
**Page 2 of 2**

**Jefferson Thomas** served as president of the student council and was an outstanding track athlete at Dunbar Junior High in Little Rock. He gave up those activities to attend Central High. He, along with Carlotta Walls, graduated from Central in 1960. Today he is an accountant with the U.S. Department of Defense living in Anaheim, California.

**Carlotta Walls LaNier** was the youngest of the Little Rock Nine. She graduated from Central High along with Jefferson Thomas in 1960. She earned a B.A. from the University of Northern Colorado. In 1968, she married Ira LaNier in Denver, Colorado. She and her family still live in Colorado, where she works as a real estate agent.

**Terrence Roberts** entered Central High as a junior. He earned a B.A. from California State University–Los Angeles, a master's degree from UCLA, and a Ph.D. in psychology from Southern Illinois University. He heads the masters in psychology program at Antioch University in Los Angeles.

**Thelma Mothershed-Wair** earned a master's degree in guidance counseling and worked as an educator in the East St. Louis school system for 28 years before retiring in 1994. She now does volunteer work in her community, including teaching survival skills at a homeless shelter.

**Minnijean Brown Trickey** was expelled from Central High in February 1958, after several incidents, including one in which she dumped a bowl of chili on a student in the school cafeteria. She stayed with the family of psychologist Kenneth Clark in New York City until she graduated from high school. She later earned a B.A. from Southern Illinois University. She and her husband moved to Canada after she graduated and raised six children on a farm. The family now lives in Maryland.

**Elizabeth Eckford** still lives in Little Rock. She served in the U.S. Army and worked as a journalist. In 1974, she returned to the home in which she grew up and is now a part-time social worker and mother of two sons. Eckford, who has a degree in history, serves on the board of the Central High Museum and Visitors Center near the school.

**Gloria Ray Karlmark** graduated from Illinois Technical College and earned a postgraduate degree in Sweden. She and her husband live in Europe, where she has worked as an executive officer of a Dutch company and the publisher of a European computer magazine.

**Reproducible 3.2**
**Page 1 of 3**

### "I am Elizabeth Eckford ..."

I am part of group that became known as the Little Rock Nine. Prior to the segregation of Central, there had been one high school for whites, Central High School, and one high school for blacks, Dunbar. I expected that there may be something more available to me at Central that was not available at Dunbar; that there might be more courses I could pursue; that there were more options available. I was not prepared for what actually happened.

I was more concerned about what I would wear, whether we could finish my dress in time.... What I was wearing, was that okay? Would it look good? The night before when the governor went on television [September 2] and announced that he had called out the Arkansas National Guard, I thought he had done this to insure the protection of all the students. We did not have a telephone. So, inevitably we were not contacted to let us know that Daisy Bates of NAACP had arranged for some ministers to accompany the students in a group. And so it was I that arrived alone.

On the morning of September 4th, my mother was doing what she usually did. My mother was making sure everybody's hair looked right and everybody had lunch money and notebooks and things. But she did finally get quiet and we had family prayer. I remember my father walking back and forth. My father worked at night and normally he would have been asleep at that time, but he was awake and he was walking back and forth chomping on a cigar that wasn't lit.

I expected I would go to school as I did before on a city bus. So, I walked a few blocks to the bus stop, got on the bus, and rode to within two blocks of the school. I got off the bus and I noticed along the street that there were many more cars than usual. And I remember hearing the murmur of a crowd. But, when I got to the corner where the school was, I was reassured seeing these solders circling school grounds. And I saw students going to school. I saw the guards break ranks as students approached the sidewalks so that they could pass through to get to school.

CONTINUED

**Reproducible 3.2**
**Page 2 of 3**

And I approached the guards at the corner, as I had seen other students do, they closed ranks. So, I thought maybe I am not supposed to enter at this point. So, I walked further down the line of guards to where there was another sidewalk and I attempted to pass through there. But when I stepped up, they crossed rifles. And again I said to myself maybe I'm supposed to go down to where the main entrance is. So I walked toward the center of the street and when I got to about the middle and I approached the guard he directed me across the street into the crowd. It was only then that I realized that they were barring me so that I wouldn't go to school.

As I stepped out into the street, the people who had been across the street start surging forward behind me. So, I headed in the opposite direction to where there was another bus stop. Safety to me meant getting to the bus stop. I think I sat there for a long time before the bus came. In the meantime, people were screaming behind me. What I would have described as a crowd before, to my ears sounded like a mob.

CONTINUED

**Reproducible 3.2**
**Page 3 of 3**

1.  Study the photographs carefully. Describe what you see. Where are people standing? How are they relating to one another? If you were there, what sounds might you hear? If you were a reporter, whom would you want to interview? What questions might you ask?

2.  Elizabeth tells her story of her first day at Central High School in Little Rock from her point of view. Choose one person in the photograph above and write a short story about how that individual happened to be at Central High School that morning. What choices did that individual make?

# LESSON 2: The Choices the Leaders Made

**Central Question:** How do the choices people make, individually and collectively, shape a society?

## Getting Started

Ask students why they think Elizabeth Eckford's first day at school turned out so differently than she and others expected. What went wrong? Explain that in this lesson students will examine the choices made by two leaders in the days immediately before and after school opened in Little Rock. Those leaders are Arkansas Governor Orval E. Faubus and U.S. President Dwight D. Eisenhower. Encourage students to pay careful attention to:

- The way each leader defined the crisis in Little Rock
- The powers and responsibilities of each leader according to the Constitution
- The individuals, groups, and ideas that shaped each leader's decisions
- The consequences of those choices.

## Background Information

For 17 days, the Arkansas National Guard kept the Little Rock Nine from entering Central High. During that period, a number of people tried to resolve the crisis. Both those who favored integration and those who opposed it saw the crisis as a constitutional issue — a question of federalism. Does a governor or any other state official have the right to disobey a decision issued by the U.S. Supreme Court?

In a federal system, some rights belong to both the nation and the states; others belong only to the nation or only to the states. The line between the nation's powers and those that belong solely to the states is not always clear-cut. Those who argue in favor of a strong central government often point to Article VI of the Constitution. It states that the Constitution, federal laws, and treaties approved by the Senate are *supreme* — that is, they are the highest law of the land. It also states that members of all three branches of government at both the state and national level are required to support the U.S. Constitution. Those who favor states rights often focus on the 10th Amendment to the Constitution, which says that all powers not given to the federal government or specifically denied to the states belong to the states.

On September 14, President Eisenhower and Governor Faubus met in Newport, Rhode Island, to privately work out their differences. At that meeting, the president reminded the governor of his responsibilities under the Constitution. Eisenhower did not want Faubus to remove the troops; he wanted the governor to use the National Guard to protect the nine students so that integration could proceed as planned.

While the two men were talking, lawyers for the NAACP were in court on behalf of the nine African American students. The lawyers argued that the governor was interfering with the students' right to attend school. If he felt that they were in danger, as he indicated in his speech, his obligation under the law was to protect them rather than side with the mob. On Friday, September 20, Federal Judge Ronald Davies ordered Faubus to stop blocking integration. To President Eisenhower's disgust, Faubus responded by withdrawing the National Guard. The Little Rock Nine were left defenseless.

The following Monday, about 100 local police officers placed wooden barricades around Central High as more than a thousand angry white men and women from Arkansas and surrounding states gathered in front of the building. To avoid the crowd, the African American students entered the school through a side door. When word got out that the students were in the building, the crowd went on a rampage — attacking journalists, breaking windows, smashing doors, and nearly lynching the Little Rock Nine. The police had to smuggle the African American students out of the building for their own safety. Early the next morning, Woodrow W. Mann, the mayor of Little Rock, sent a telegraph to President Eisenhower asking for federal help in keeping the peace.

That evening President Eisenhower addressed the nation on television and radio. He told Americans, "The very basis of our individual rights and freedoms rests upon the certainty that the President and the Executive Branch of government will support and insure the carrying out of the decisions of the Federal courts, even, when necessary, with all the means at the President's command." He added: "Mob rule cannot be allowed to override the decisions of our courts." He then ordered the 101st Airborne Division to Little Rock.

The next day, September 25, U.S. soldiers escorted the Little Rock Nine to school. This time, Melba Pattillo, one of the Little Rock Nine, recalls, "I went in not through the side doors, but up the front stairs, and there was a feeling of pride and hope that yes, this is the United States; yes, there is a reason I salute the flag; and it's going to be okay."

**Note:** If you wish to add a mini-lesson on the impact federalism had on the way the two men responded to the crisis, you may wish to use the optional documents at the end of Part 3. They include:
- Eisenhower's letter to Faubus in response to a telegram received from the governor on September 5
- Eisenhower's notes on his meeting with Faubus at Newport, Rhode Island
- Press releases the two men issued independently at the end of the meeting
- The mayor's telegram requesting federal intervention.

**Activity: Defining Positions**

Explain to students that millions of Americans watched the crisis in Little Rock unfold on television. These news clips were later made into a film. Show students "Fighting Back" from *Eyes on the Prize* beginning with Eisenhower's press conference and ending just after the rioting on September 4 (about six minutes). As students watch, encourage them to use the timeline (**Reproducible 3.3**) to keep track of events and highlight key moments in the story. Have them pay particular attention to the choices made by President Dwight D. Eisenhower and Governor Orval E. Faubus of Arkansas.

After showing the first clip from the video, distribute **Reproducible 3.4**. To introduce the activity, you may wish to draw a horizontal line on the board. At one end, write "Integration" and the other "Segregation." Ask students to use the video to identify where each man seemed to stand in the spring and summer of 1957. (Both men could probably be placed in the middle of the line or leaning slightly toward segregation.) Ask students to list the pressures on Faubus to change his stand. According to the video, what choice did he make on September 2?

Ask students to work with a partner to fill in the second part of the reproducible to reflect the decision Governor Faubus announced on September 2, as well as his response to the mob that gathered at the high school on September 4. How did those events affect where Faubus stood on the issue of integration? Have partners find a place for Faubus on the line. Then ask them to place Eisenhower on that same line. To what extent did Faubus's action affect Eisenhower's position?

Show Part 2 of the video from the lawsuit filed by the NAACP to Eisenhower's decision to send in troops and Faubus's reaction to that decision (about six minutes). Again, have students locate each leader's position on the spectrum and identify the people and events that informed that decision.

**Activity: Defining the Role of Public Opinion**

Ask students to define the term *public opinion* (the beliefs of ordinary citizens about an event, issue, or idea). What part does public opinion play in a democracy? How do leaders learn what people think about an issue? Should leaders take into account public opinion when they make a decision? Ask students how public opinion in Arkansas affected the choices Faubus made. How did it shape the decisions Eisenhower made? Have students read an essay by Jesus Colon (Part 1, Lesson 2, **Reproducible 1.2**) in 1957 (**Reproducible 3.5**) and answer the questions at the end of the reading.

After students have discussed their answers with a partner, ask if their opinion would change if the letters sent to the White House were in support of Faubus rather than the Little Rock Nine. To focus the discussion, use an activity known as the "Last Word." Divide the class into groups of five and ask one person in each group to take no more than a minute to give their opinion on the question. Then have each person in the group, one by one, respond in 30 seconds or less to what the first person said. When everyone has had a say, the first person to speak has the "last word." They can take 30 seconds to respond to the other speakers. To continue the discussion, ask a second person to lead a round of discussion.

### Activity: Evaluating a Decision

Distribute **Reproducible 3.6** and ask students to read Eisenhower's address to the nation. Have them underline the sentences that justify his decision. Then ask students to work with a partner on a headline that summarizes the choice Eisenhower made. (Remind students that headlines summarize a story in 12 words or less and usually contain a subject and a verb.) What factors pushed Eisenhower from a neutral position on *Brown* to one in which he actively enforced integration? Who did the President listen to? Who should a president listen to?

### Homework Activity: Weighing the Consequences of Eisenhower's Decision

Distribute **Reproducible 3.7**. Ask students to compare and contrast the way Melba Pattillo felt on September 23 with the way she felt on September 26. What made the difference? Have students write a paragraph describing how the Little Rock Nine and their parents viewed Eisenhower's decision. How did the way he defined his role as president affect them personally?

### Discussion Suggestions

- What constitutional issue was at the heart of the crisis in Little Rock? What do you think would have happened had Eisenhower allowed Faubus to defy a federal law or a ruling of the U.S. Supreme Court?
- How do you think seeing the crisis in Little Rock unfold on television shaped the way Americans viewed integration?
- What are some of the ways individuals and groups tried to influence the decisions that Governor Faubus and President Eisenhower faced in the fall of 1957? Which methods were most effective?
- How did the mob that attacked the African American students affect the choices each leader made? How did the mob shape public opinion?

### Writing Suggestions

- What acts of courage did you witness in the news clips you watched from *Eyes on the Prize*? Which one impressed you the most?
- If you had been a reporter at Central High School on the morning of September 23, 1957, whom would you have interviewed? What questions would you have liked to ask?
- What do you think will happen next in this story?

# Timeline

As you watch film clips and read the information provided in this part of the unit, highlight the events that you think are central to the story. Which event marks a turning point in the story? A *turning point* is an event that marks an important change of course or an event on which important developments depend.

**May 24, 1955**       The School Board votes unanimously to adopt Superintendent Virgil Blossom's plan of gradual integration. Integration will start in September 1957 at the high school level and add lower grades over a period of six years.

**February 8, 1956**       The NAACP files suit on behalf of 33 African American children.

**August 28, 1956**       Federal Judge John E. Miller dismisses the NAACP suit, declaring the Little Rock School Board acted in "utmost good faith."

**Spring 1957**       The School Board determines that 517 Black students live in the Central High district. Following interviews with the superintendent and staff, 17 are selected for the first year of integration at Central. Eight later decide to remain at Horace Mann High School.

**August 27, 1957**       A member of the Mother's League of Central High is granted an injunction* to temporarily stop school integration.

**August 30, 1957**       Federal District Judge Ronald Davies overturns the injunction and orders integration to proceed as planned.

**September 2, 1957**       Governor Orval Faubus sends the Arkansas National Guard to Central High School to "preserve the peace and avoid violence."

CONTINUED

* A court order that stops a person from doing something or requires a person to do something.

**Reproducible 3.3**
**Page 2 of 2**

September 3, 1957    Judge Davies orders desegregation to begin September 4.

September 4, 1957    The nine Black students try to enter Central High only to be turned away by the National Guard.

September 10, 1957    The U.S. Department of Justice files an injunction against Governor Faubus to force him to obey Judge Davies's desegregation order.

September 14, 1957    President Dwight D. Eisenhower meets with Governor Faubus in Newport, Rhode Island, to discuss desegregation in Little Rock.

September 20, 1957    Judge Davies orders Governor Faubus to remove the National Guard. Faubus announces he will obey the order in a televised speech but asks African Americans to stay away from the high school.

September 23, 1957    When a mob outside the school learns the African Americans students have entered Central High, riots follow. The African American students are taken out of the school through a side door.

September 24, 1957    Little Rock Mayor Woodrow Mann asks President Eisenhower for help in maintaining order. The President announces that he is sending 1,000 members of the 101st Airborne Division to Little Rock and federalizes the Arkansas National Guard.

September 25, 1957    Federal troops escort the Little Rock Nine to classes at Central High.

**Reproducible 3.4**
**Page 1 of 2**

# Identifying Decisions

### 1. Spring and summer 1957

Based on what you saw in *Eyes on the Prize*, what pressures do President Eisenhower and governors like Orval Faubus of Arkansas face as school boards across the nation carry out the Supreme Court's decision in *Brown v. Board of Education*? List the pressures on each man in the space below or on a separate sheet of paper.

Eisenhower                                                      Faubus

_____                          _____

_____                          _____

_____                          _____

_____                          _____

Based on what you saw and heard in the video, where on the line below would you place President Eisenhower on September 1, 1957? Where would you place Governor Faubus?

_____

Integration                                                                                    Segregation

### 2. September 2–4, 1957

Based on what you saw in the news clips from *Eyes on the Prize*, what pressures does each leader face after the speech Faubus gave on the night of September 2, 1957? List them in the space below or on a separate sheet of paper.

Eisenhower                                                      Faubus

_____                          _____

_____                          _____

_____                          _____

_____                          _____

CONTINUED

**Reproducible 3.4**
**Page 2 of 2**

Based on what you saw and heard in the news clips from *Eyes on the Prize*, where on the line below would you place President Eisenhower on September 4, 1957? Where would you place Governor Faubus?

_____

Integration                                                                                    Segregation

Based on what you saw in the news clips from *Eyes on the Prize*, what pressures does each leader face <u>after</u> Faubus removed the National Guard on September 20, 1957, and the Little Rock Nine entered Central High School on September 23? List them in the space below or on a separate sheet of paper.

Eisenhower                                                          Faubus

_____                          _____

_____                          _____

_____                          _____

_____                          _____

3.  **September 20–24, 1957**

Based on what you saw and heard in the news clips from *Eyes on the Prize*, where on the line below would you place Eisenhower on September 24, 1957? Where would you place Governor Faubus?

_____

Integration                                                                                    Segregation

4. How do you account for the shifts in the positions of each leader? Underline the factor or factors that seemed to have the greatest impact on each man.

**Reproducible 3.5**

# Shaping Public Opinion

In 1957, Jesus Colon [Part 1] wrote a newspaper column about the Little Rock Nine. In it he describes what a friend in New York did a few days after Governor Faubus called out the National Guard.

> Joe took a rough piece of paper from the factory and wrote a request to the President of the United States to use his federal and military powers to keep open the doors of the high school to the Negro children. Joe then asked the sixty workers in his shop to sign their names to the request. About forty of them signed. Then Joe put the whole thing in an envelope and sent it to President Eisenhower. Joe is a white worker. Can you imagine the effect in the White House if other Joes in thousands of other factories and offices all over the nation would have done the same? Enough said.*

1.     How would you answer Colon's question?

2.     What is Colon suggesting about the way he and other Americans could influence the decision the president made?

3.     What is your opinion of Joe's idea? Should the president of the United States be influenced by the opinions of ordinary citizens?

4.     What other ways might ordinary citizens make their views known? How do you make your voice heard?

---

* Jesus Colon, *A Puerto Rican in New York*. Mainstream, 1961.

**Reproducible 3.6**
**Page 1 of 2**

# An Address to the Nation

Read the speech that President Eisenhower gave to the nation on September 24, 1957. Underline the sentences that reveal the things he took into account in making his decision. Then answer the questions on page 2.

*My Fellow Citizens....* I must speak to you about the serious situation that has arisen in Little Rock.... This morning the mob again gathered in front of the Central High School of Little Rock, obviously for the purpose of again preventing the carrying out of the court's order relating to the admission of Negro children to that school.

Whenever normal agencies prove inadequate to the task and it becomes necessary for the executive branch of the federal government to use its powers and authority to uphold federal courts, the president's responsibility is inescapable.

In accordance with that responsibility, I have today issued an Executive Order directing the use of troops under federal authority to aid in the execution of federal law at Little Rock, Arkansas....

As you know, the Supreme Court of the United States has decided that separate public educational facilities for the races are inherently unequal and therefore compulsory school segregation laws are unconstitutional.... During the past several years, many communities in our southern states have instituted public school plans for gradual progress in the enrollment and attendance of school children of all races in order to bring themselves into compliance with the law of the land. They thus demonstrated to the world that we are a nation in which laws, not men, are supreme. I regret to say that this truth — the cornerstone of our liberties — was not observed in this instance....

The very basis of our individual rights and freedoms rests upon the certainty that the president and the executive branch of government will support and insure the carrying out of the decisions of the federal courts, even, when necessary, with all the means at the president's command....

Mob rule cannot be allowed to override the decisions of our courts.

Now, let me make it very clear that federal troops are not being used to relieve local and state authorities of their primary duty to preserve the peace and order of the community....

CONTINUED

**Reproducible 3.6**
**Page 2 of 2**

The proper use of the powers of the executive branch to enforce the orders of a federal court is limited to extraordinary and compelling circumstances. Manifestly, such an extreme situation has been created in Little Rock. This challenge must be met and with such measures as will preserve to the people as a whole their lawfully protected rights in a climate permitting their free and fair exercise.

The overwhelming majority of our people in every section of the country are united in their respect for observance of the law — even in those cases where they may disagree with that law.... A foundation of our American way of life is our national respect for law.

In the South, as elsewhere, citizens are keenly aware of the tremendous disservice that has been done to the people of Arkansas in the eyes of the nation, and that has been done to the nation in the eyes of the world.

At a time when we face grave situations abroad because of the hatred that communism bears toward a system of government based on human rights, it would be difficult to exaggerate the harm that is being done to the prestige and influence, and indeed to the safety, of our nation and the world....

And so, with deep confidence, I call upon the citizens of the state of Arkansas to assist in bringing an immediate end to all interference with the law and its processes. If resistance to the federal court orders ceases at once,... Little Rock will return to its normal habits of peace and order and a blot upon the fair name and high honor of our nation in the world will be removed. Thus will be restored the image of America and of all its parts as one nation, indivisible, with liberty and justice for all.

1. How does Eisenhower's view of his responsibilities as president affect the choice he makes?

2. What does he see as the responsibilities of every American citizen?

**Reproducible 3.7**
**Page 1 of 4**

# The Impact of a Decision

In her book *Warriors Don't Cry*, Melba Pattillo describes her feelings on September 23, 1957 — the day she and the other eight African American students had to sneak out of the school to save their lives:

> What I felt inside was stark raving fear — terrible, wrenching, awful fear.... There are no words for how I felt inside. I had known no pain like that because I did not know what I had done wrong. You see, when you're fifteen years old and someone's going to hit you or hurt you, you want to know what you did wrong. Although I knew the differences between black and white, I didn't know the penalties one paid for being black at that time.

Three days later, she wrote in the diary she kept in high school:

> It's Thursday, September 26, 1957. Now I have a bodyguard. I know very well that the President didn't send those soldiers just to protect me but to show support for an idea — the idea that a [state] government can't ignore federal laws. Still, I feel especially cared about because the guard is there. If he wasn't there, I'd hear more of the voices of those people who say I'm a nigger ... that I'm not valuable, that I have no right to be alive.

Melba's mother shared her daughter's feelings. On September 30, she and the parents of the other eight African American students sent a telegram to the president. Read the telegram (pages 2–4) and the president's letter in response to the telegram. (You may find the telegram a little hard to read unless you know that there are no punctuation marks in a telegram. The word *stop* is used to show the end of a sentence.)

1.     What do the parents want the president to know?


2.     What impact has his decision had on them and their children?


3.     What does the president want the parents to know?


4.     What do Melba's diary entry, the telegram, and Eisenhower's letter suggest is the role of a president in a democracy?

CONTINUED

RECEIVED
OCT - 7 1957

The White GENERAL FILES
Washington

WA037 NL PD

LITTLE ROCK ARK SEP 30    1957 OCT 1  AM 7 43

THE PRESIDENT

THE WHITE HOUSE

WE THE PARENTS OF NINE NEGRO CHILDREN ENROLLED AT LITTLE
ROCK CENTRAL HIGH SCHOOL WANT YOU TO KNOW THAT YOUR
ACTION IN SAFE GUARDING THEIR RIGHTS HAVE STRENGTHENED
OUR FAITH IN DEMOCRACY STOP NOW AS NEVER BEFORE WE HAVE
AN ABIDING FEELING OF BELONGING AND PURPOSEFULNESS STOP
WE BELIEVE THAT FREEDOM AND EQUALITY WITH WHICH ALL MEN

ARE ENDOWED AT BIRTH CAN BE MAINTAINED ONLY THROUGH
FREEDOM AND EQUALITY OF OPPORTUNITY FOR SELF DEVELOPMENT
GROWTH AND PURPOSEFUL CITIZENSHIP STOP WE BELIEVE THAT
THE DEGREE TO WHICH PEOPLE EVERYWHERE REALIZE AND ACCEPT
THIS CONCEPT WILL DETERMINE IN A LARGE MEASURE AMERICAS
TRUE GROWTH AND TRUE GREATNESS STOP YOU HAVE DEMONSTRATED
ADMIRABLY TO US THE NATION AND THE WORLD HOW PROFOUNDLY
YOU BELIEVE IN THIS CONCEPT STOP FOR THIS WE ARE DEEPLY
GRATEFUL AND RESPECTFULLY EXTEND TO YOU OUR HEARTFELT
AND LASTING THANKS STOP MAY THE ALMIGHTY AND ALL WISE

CONTINUED

FATHER OF US ALL BLESS GUIDE AND KEEP YOU ALWASY
OSCAR ECKFORD JR 4405 WEST 18TH LOTHAIRE S GREEN 1224
WEST 21ST ST JUANITA WALLS 1500 VALENTINE W B BROWN
1117 RINGO LOIS M PATTILLO 1121 CROSS H C RAY 2111
CROSS ELLIS THOMAS 1214 WEST 20TH W L ROBERTS 2301
HOWARD H L MOTHERSHED 1313 CHESTER.

CONTINUED

RECEIVED
OCT - 5 1957
CENTRAL FILES

October 4, 1957

PERSONAL

Dear Mr. Brown:

I deeply appreciate your September thirtieth telegram,
signed also by other parents. The supreme law of our
land has been clearly defined by the Supreme Court.
To support and defend the Constitution of the United
States is my solemn oath as your President -- a pledge
which imposes upon me the responsibility to see that
the laws of our country are faithfully executed. I shall
continue to discharge that responsibility in the interest
of all Americans today, as well as to preserve our free
institutions of government for the sake of Americans
yet unborn.

I believe that America's heart goes out to you and your
children in your present ordeal. In the course of our
country's progress toward equality of opportunity, you
have shown dignity and courage in circumstances which
would daunt citizens of lesser faith.

With best wishes to you,

Sincerely,

(sgd) DWIGHT D. EISENHOWER

Mr. W. B. Brown
1117 Ringo Street
Little Rock
Arkansas

PERSONAL

(Sent to Mr. David H. Stephens, Chief Postal Inspector, Room 3426,
Post Office Dept., for delivery)

THE WHITE HOUSE

U. S. Naval Base
Newport, Rhode Island

THE PRESIDENT TODAY SENT THE
FOLLOWING TELEGRAM TO THE
HONORABLE ORVAL E. FAUBUS,
THE GOVERNOR OF ARKANSAS

The Honorable Orval E. Faubus
Governor of Arkansas
Little Rock, Arkansas

Your telegram received requesting my assurance of understanding
of and cooperation in the course of action you have taken on school
integration recommended by the Little Rock School Board and
ordered by the United States District Court pursuant to the mandate
of the United States Supreme Court.

When I became President, I took an oath to support and defend the
Constitution of the United States. The only assurance I can give
you is that the Federal Constitution will be upheld by me by every
legal means at my command.

There is no basis of fact to the statements you make in your telegram
that Federal authorities have been considering taking you into custody
or that telephone lines to your Executive Mansion have been tapped
by any agency of the Federal Government.

At the request of Judge Davies, the Department of Justice is
presently collecting facts as to interference with or failure to
comply with the District Court's order. You and other state
officials -- as well as the National Guard which, of course, is
uniformed, armed and partially sustained by the Government --
will, I am sure, give full cooperation to the United States District
Court.

Dwight D. Eisenhower

DIARY
Notes dictated by the President on October 8, 1957 concerning visit of
Governor Orval Faubus of Arkansas to Little Rock on September 14, 1957.

Interview was held in the President's tiny office at the Naval Station at
Newport. At the beginning of what was approximately a two hour
session, the President and the Governor were alone in the President's
office for about twenty minutes. They then adjourned to acw's office,
which was larger.

"What he had to say was pretty well represented in the press releases
given out that day (attached). Governor Faubus protested again and
again he was a law abiding citizen, that he was a veteran, fought in the
war, and that everybody recognizes that the Federal law is supreme to
State law. So I suggested to him that he go home and not necessarily
withdraw his National Guard troops, but just change their orders to say
that having been assured that there was no attempt to do anything except
to obey the Courts and that the Federal government was not trying to
do anything that had not been already agreed to by the School Board
and directed by the Courts; that he should tell the Guard to continue to
preserve order but to allow the Negro children to attend Central High
School. I pointed out at that time he was due to appear the following
Friday, the 20th, before the Court to determine whether an injunction
was to be issued. In any event, I urged him to take this action
promptly whereupon the Justice Department would go to the Court and
ask that the Governor not be brought into Court. I further said that
I did not believe it was beneficial to anybody to have a trial of strength
between the President and a Governor because in any area where the
Federal government had assumed jurisdiction and this was upheld by
the Supreme Court, there could be only one outcome -- that is, the
State would lose, and I did not want to see any Governor humiliated.

"He seemed to be very appreciative of this attitude and I got definitely
the understanding that he was going back to Arkansas to act within a
matter of hours to revoke his orders to the Guard to prevent re-entry
of the Negro children into the school.

"He told me of his war experiences and vigorously asserted his deep
feelings of loyalty and dedication to the Federal government, and re-
peated several times that he had shown respect for the law in all his
actions.

"After some 20 minutes of personal conference, we invited Governor
Adams and Brooks Hays, and later, the Attorney General, to join us.
The ensuing conversation was generally along the same lines as he had
talked to me in private."

- - - - - - - - - - - - - - - - - - - - - - - - - - - - - - - - - - - - - - - -

## THE WHITE HOUSE

## U. S. NAVAL BASE
## NEWPORT, RHODE ISLAND

## STATEMENT BY THE PRESIDENT

At the request of Governor Faubus of Arkansas I met with him this morning in a constructive discussion regarding the carrying out of the orders of the Federal Court in the matter of the high schools of Little Rock.

The Governor stated his intention to respect the decisions of the United States District Court and to give his full cooperation in carrying out his responsibilities in respect to these decisions. In so doing, I recognize the inescapable responsibility resting upon the Governor to preserve law and order in his state.

I am gratified by his constructive and cooperative attitude at our meeting. I have assured the Governor of the cooperation of Federal officials. I was pleased to hear from the Governor of the progress already made in the elimination of segregation in other activities in the State of Arkansas.

I am sure it is the desire of the Governor not only to observe the supreme law of the land but to use the influence of his office in orderly progress of the plans which are already the subject of the order of the Court.

###### 

Over

## STATEMENT BY THE GOVERNOR OF ARKANSAS

The President and I had a friendly and constructive discussion of the problem of compliance with Court orders respecting the high schools of Little Rock.

This trip to Newport has been worthwhile from my point of view.

I recognize that the situation calls for clarification, and I have assured the President of my desire to cooperate with him in carrying out the duties resting upon both of us under the Federal Constitution. In addition, I must harmonize my actions under the Constitution of Arkansas with the requirements of the Constitution of the United States.

I have never expressed any personal opinion regarding the Supreme Court decision of 1954 which ordered integration. That is not relevant. That decision is the law of the land and must be obeyed.

At the same time it is evident even from the language of the decision itself that changes necessitated by the Court orders cannot be accomplished overnight. The people of Little Rock are law-abiding and I know that they expect to obey valid Court orders. In this they shall have my support.

In so doing it is my responsibility to protect the people from violence in any form. As I interpret the President's public statements, the national Administration has no thought of challenging this fact. In meeting this obligation, it is essential that, in proceeding to implement the orders of the Court, the complexities of integration be patiently understood by all those in Federal authority.

When I assured the President, as I have already done, that I expect to accept the decision of the Courts, I entertained the hope that the Department of Justice and the Federal Juciciary will act with understanding and patience in discharging their duties.

# # # # #

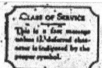

WESTERN UNION
TELEGRAM
W. P. MARSHALL, President

CLASS OF SERVICE
This is a fast message unless its deferred character is indicated by the proper symbol.

SYMBOLS
DL=Day Letter
NL=Night Letter
LT=International Letter Telegram

1201

The filing time shown in the date line on domestic telegrams is STANDARD TIME at point of origin. Time of receipt is STANDARD TIME at point of destination

1201 SEP 24 AM 10 37

NP328 P LRA006 LONG   PRD RX=LITTLEROCK ARK 24 916AMC=

PRESIDENT DWIGHT D EISENHOWER=

THE WHITE HOUSE NEWPORT RI=

THE IMMEDIATE NEED FOR FEDERAL TROOPS IS URGENT. THE MOB
IS MUCH LARGER IN NUMBERS AT 8AM THAN AT ANY TIME
YESTERDAY PEOPLE ARE CONVERGING ON THE SCENE FROM ALL
DIRECTIONS MOB IS ARMED AND ENGAGING IN FISTICUFFS AND
OTHER ACTS OF VIOLENCE. SITUATION IS OUT OF CONTROL AND
POLICE CANNOT DISPERSE THE MOB I AM PLEADING TO YOU AS
PRESIDENT OF THE UNITED STATES IN THE INTEREST OF
HUMANITY LAW AND ORDER AND BECAUSE OF DEMOCRACY WORLD

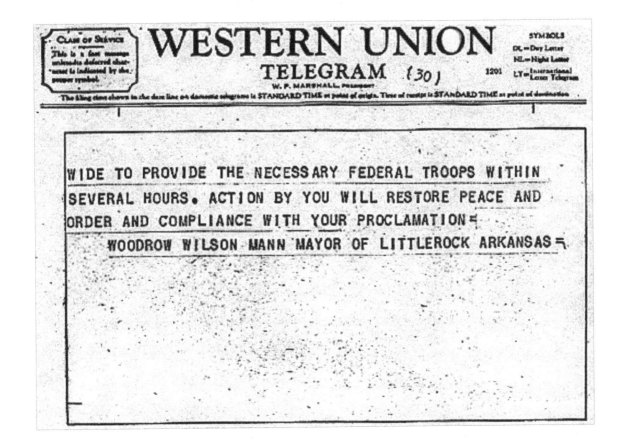

WIDE TO PROVIDE THE NECESSARY FEDERAL TROOPS WITHIN

SEVERAL HOURS. ACTION BY YOU WILL RESTORE PEACE AND

ORDER AND COMPLIANCE WITH YOUR PROCLAMATION=

WOODROW WILSON MANN MAYOR OF LITTLEROCK ARKANSAS=

# LESSON 3: The Choices the Media Made

**Central Question:** How do the choices people make, individually and collectively, shape a society?

## Getting Started

You may wish to begin by discussing the homework assignment in the previous lesson. Ask students to share with a partner their responses to the quotations from Melba Pattillo's book, the telegram sent by the parents of the Little Rock Nine, and the president's response. What do these opinions add to our understanding of the role of the president in a democracy? Then ask students to consider what role ordinary citizens play in a democracy. Remind students that the Bill of Rights — the first ten amendments to the Constitution — spells out the rights of every American. Those rights include freedom of speech, the right to organize a protest, and the right to demand that the government make changes. However, each of those rights has limits.

- A person has the right to speak out on the issues of the day but *not* to start a riot.
- A person has the right to peacefully assemble — to meet openly with other citizens to protest a new law or support a candidate for public office — but *not* the right to incite a mob or destroy property.
- A person has the right to petition or formally ask the government to change a law, write a new law, or fix a problem but *not* to send hate mail.

The press (newspapers, magazines, TV, radio, and today, the Internet) has rights as well. Reporters and other journalists have the right to not only make information public but also express their opinions without fear of arrest. They do *not* have the right to print information they know is false or is likely to endanger the public. In this lesson, students will examine the role the press played during the crisis in Little Rock.

## Background Information

Journalists from every part of the United States and countries around the world came to Little Rock to report on events at Central High School. Among them were newspaper reporters, photographers, TV and radio correspondents, and camera crews. They too made decisions, and their choices helped shape the outcome. The integration of Central High School was the first civil rights story featured on television. At the time, national newscasts were 15 minutes long, and night after night, Little Rock was the lead story. Millions of people who had never been to Arkansas followed events at Central High School on TV.

Reporting the story was no easy task. The mobs attacked and viciously beat African American journalists. They also attacked some white journalists. David Halberstam, then a young reporter, writes:

> Because of the dangers, there were certain rules — a reporter never carried a notebook that he could not hide in a pocket. [One reporter's] first rule of coverage was: Never take notes in front of a crowd. It was better to dress casual than sharp. A reporter never went out on a story alone. One did not argue with the segregationists or provoke them. Whatever moral [disgust] a reporter felt about the events taking place in front of him, it was to be kept bottled up.[9]

### Activity: A Crisis Heard Around the World

Explain to students that millions of Americans followed the crisis in Little Rock on television, as did people around the world. *The Arkanasas Gazette* reprinted editorial comments about the crisis from newspapers around the world. Ask students to work with a partner to locate the countries referred to on **Reproducible 3.8** on the map that appears on page 2 of the reproducible. Encourage partners to think about why people in distant places cared about the fate of nine teenagers from Little Rock, Arkansas. How did those people affect the way the president of the United States viewed the crisis? Why do you think the editors of the Arkansas newspaper reprinted those opinions?

### Activity: What Is the Role of the Media?

Ask students to describe the job of a reporter. To what extent is a reporter an objective observer? What happens when a reporter becomes part of the story? **Reproducible 3.9** and **Reproducible 3.10** focus on two reporters who became part of the story. Have half of the class read **Reproducible 3.9** and the other half read **Reproducible 3.10**. Then have students share what they learned with a partner. What decision did each reporter make? How did his choice affect his ability to report the news? David Halberstam, a young reporter in the 1950s, writes that when Ben Fine comforted Elizabeth Eckford, he lost "his cool." "He had started to argue with the mob and the *Times* had been forced to bring him back to New York."[10] Why did *The New York Times* take Ben Fine off the story? Did his editors make the right choice? African American newspapers kept reporters like Alex Wilson on the story despite the attacks. How do you account for the choice they made? Did Wilson's editors make the right choice?

---

[9] David Halberstam, *The Fifties*. Fawcett Books, 1993, pp. 681–682.
[10] Ibid.

**Activity: Holding Up a Mirror**

Remind students of the segment from *Eyes on the Prize* in the previous lesson that shows four African American journalists being attacked by a mob. Alex Wilson is the man who was hit with a brick. Tell students that the segment is taken from a video entitled "Fighting Back." Ask students to reexamine **Reproducible 3.10.** To what extent did Wilson "fight back"? What weapons did he use to make his point? Replay the segment from *Eyes of the Prize* but this time turn off the sound. What story does the cameraman tell? To what extent is that story more powerful than Wilson's words?

Distribute **Reproducible 3.11** and ask students to read the passage and discuss the questions about the picture with a partner. In a book about the 1950s, David Halberstam wrote:

> Film was so powerful that a reporter was well advised to get out of the way and let the pictures do the talking. Certainly, that was true in Little Rock. The images were so forceful that … it was hard for people watching at home not to take sides: There they were, sitting in their living rooms in front of their own television sets watching orderly black children behaving with great dignity, trying to obtain nothing more than a decent education.[11]

What is Halberstam suggesting about the way the role of the reporter changed during the crisis in Little Rock? What part did television play in that change? How does television affect the way people view important events today? To focus the discussion, use the "Last Word" activity. Divide the class into groups of five and ask one person in each group to take no more than a minute to give their opinion on the question. Then have each person in the group, one by one, respond to what the first person said and only what that person said in 30 seconds or less. When everyone has had a say, the first person to speak has the "last word." They can take 30 seconds to respond to the other speakers. To continue the discussion, ask a second person to lead a round of discussion.

**Writing Suggestions**

- If you were to write an editorial about Little Rock, what points would you make? Which of the quotations from the foreign newspapers reflects your views?
- How much attention do you pay to events in other countries? How might you let people caught up in those events know that you care?
- What is the role of the press in a democracy? How has television affected the way stories are told? How has it affected the way stories are understood?
- Why do you think the crisis in Little Rock attracted so much attention? Would it have been as large a story if television had not yet been invented?

---

[11] Ibid.

**Reproducible 3.8**
**Page 1 of 2**

# How Did Others See Us?

Newspapers from around the world commented on the school integration crisis in Little Rock.*

**Manchester Guardian (U.K.)** — The real test is going forward in the minds of parents, teachers, local officials — all those who go to make up public opinion in Little Rock — and the real lesson is to be drawn from what has now happened at Clinton, Tenn. There Negro children are sitting in the same classroom as white, and there has been no trouble. This is true also of a number of other Southern towns that do not break into the headlines. Tension has not vanished; there will be more incidents and more noise. But the noise is the slow grind of change, and it is a healthy noise.

**Times of Indonesia** — Americans must ask themselves … whether Governor Faubus should not be hauled before the Un-American Activities Committee for alienating half the world from the United States.

**Sydney [Australia] Morning Herald** — The time for a compromise is clearly at an end. President Eisenhower's determination to "follow through" over Little Rock will be welcomed by his friends in the free world no less than by enlightened Americans.

**Mexico City El Nacional** — Racism and its methods of segregation must be [wiped out] forever. The honor of the United States and the conception itself of true civilization and Christian conscience demand it.

**Toronto [Canada] Globe & Mail** — The theory, [tirelessly] spread by the Communists for decades, that the United States is the inveterate enemy of all colored people everywhere, is likely to win much wider support than ever before. This episode illustrates a deadly contradiction in United States life and policy.

**Tokyo [Japan] News** — Nearly 100 years after the death of Abraham Lincoln, endless disputes between the two races continue everywhere. It is sometimes difficult to understand why this problem should arise in the United States, the champion of democracy.

**Manila [Philippines] Herald** — It is a test right in America's home grounds to determine how really sincere the American people are in their avowals of equal justice and fair play – a doctrine repeatedly dinned into the ears of their allies by American leaders.

CONTINUED

*Reprinted from the *Arkansas Gazette*, September 23, 1957.

# World: Countries

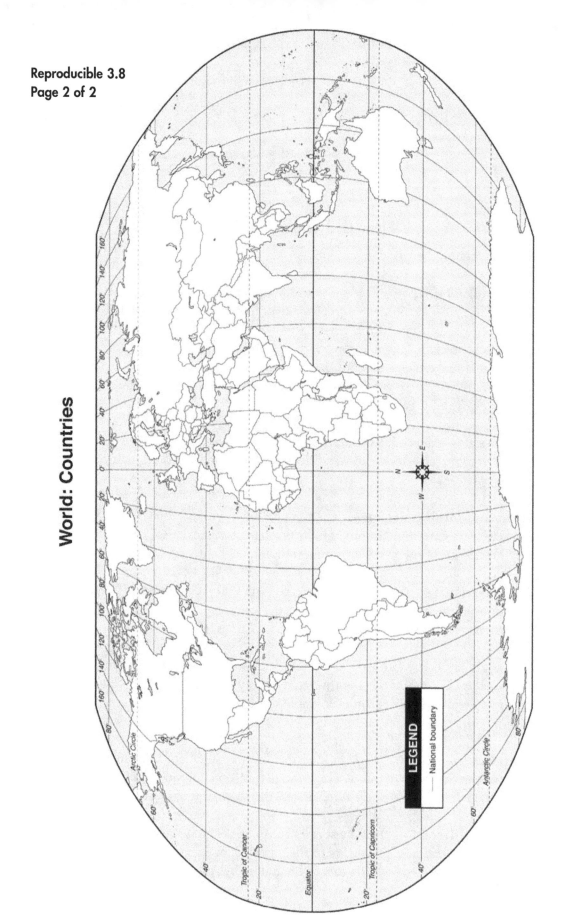

LEGEND
National boundary

**Reproducible 3.9**
**Page 1 of 2**

### "They Spat in My Face"

In her book, Daisy Bates, president of the Arkansas branch of the NAACP, reported a conversation with Dr. Benjamin Fine, the education editor of *The New York Times*. He was among the first reporters to cover the Little Rock story. Fine came to her house a few days after the National Guard kept Elizabeth Eckford from entering the school. Bates quotes Fine as saying:

"I was standing in front of the school that day. Suddenly there was a shout — 'They're here! The niggers are coming!' I saw a sweet little girl who looked about fifteen, walking alone. She tried several times to pass through the guards. The last time she tried, they put their bayonets in front of her. When they did this, she became panicky. For a moment she just stood there trembling. Then she seemed to calm down and started walking toward the bus stop with the mob baying at her heels like a pack of hounds. The women were shouting, 'Get her! Lynch her!' The men were yelling, 'Go home, you bastard of a black bitch!' She finally made it to the bus stop and sat down on the bench. I sat down beside her and said, 'I'm a reporter from *The New York Times*. May I have your name?' She just sat there, her head down. Tears were streaming down her cheeks from under her sunglasses. Daisy, I don't know what made me put my arm around her, lifting her chin, saying, 'Don't let them see you cry.' Maybe she reminded me of my fifteen-year-old daughter, Jill.

"There must have been five hundred around us by this time. I vaguely remember someone hollering, 'Get a rope and drag her over to this tree.' Suddenly I saw a white-haired, kind-faced woman fighting her way through the mob. She looked at Elizabeth and then screamed at the mob, 'Leave this child alone! Why are you tormenting her? Six months from now, you will hang your heads in shame.' The mob shouted, 'Another nigger-lover. Get out of here!' The woman, who I found out later was Mrs. Grace Lorch, the wife of Dr. Lee Lorch, professor at Philander Smith College, turned to me and said, 'We have to do something. Let's try to get a cab.'

CONTINUED

**Reproducible 3.9**
**Page 2 of 2**

"We took Elizabeth across the street to the drugstore. I remained on the sidewalk with Elizabeth while Mrs. Lorch tried to enter the drugstore to call a cab. But the hoodlums slammed the door in her face and wouldn't let her in. She pleaded with them to call a cab for the child. They closed in on her saying, 'Get out of here, you bitch!' Just then the city bus came. Mrs. Lorch and Elizabeth got on. Elizabeth must have been in a state of shock. She never uttered a word. When the bus pulled away, the mob closed in around me. 'We saw you put your arm around that little bitch. Now it's your turn.' A drab, middle-aged woman said viciously, 'Grab him and kick him in the balls!' A girl I had seen hustling in one of the local bars screamed, 'A dirty New York Jew! Get him!' A man asked me, 'Are you a Jew?' I said, 'Yes.' He then said to the mob, 'Let him be! We'll take care of him later.'

"The irony of it all, Daisy, is that during all this time the national guardsmen made no effort to protect Elizabeth or help me. Instead, they threatened to have me arrested for inciting to riot."*

1.      Why does Benjamin Fine think he tried to help Elizabeth Eckford?
Did he do the right thing?

2.      What is the danger in a journalist becoming a part of the story they are reporting?

3.      David Halberstam, a young reporter in the 1950s, wrote that when Ben Fine comforted Elizabeth Eckford, he lost "his cool." "He had started to argue with the mob and the *Times* had been forced to bring him back to New York."** Halberstam maintains that however a reporter "feels about the events taking place in front of him, it has to be kept bottled up." What is he suggesting about the role of a reporter? To what extent do you think Fine would agree? Did the *Times* do the right thing when it replaced Fine with another reporter?

---

* Daisy Bates, *The Long Shadow of Little Rock: A Memoir.* David McKay Company, Inc., 1962, pp. 69–71.
** David Halberstam, *The Fifties.* Fawcett Books, 1993, pp. 681–682.

**Reproducible 3.10**
**Page 1 of 2**

## "I Decided Not to Run"

The coverage of the Little Rock crisis in *Eyes on the Prize* shows the mob attacking four African American journalists — reporters Alex Wilson of the *Memphis Tri-State Defender*, James Hicks of the *Amsterdam News*, Moses J. Newsom of the Afro-American newspapers and photographer Earl Davy of Little Rock. Wilson was the reporter who was hit with a brick. Shortly after he was attacked, Wilson wrote about what happened to him on the morning that the crowd at Central High School turned violent and the choice he made that day:

> The disgraceful incident ... occurred about 8:20 a.m. Monday, near the 16th and Park Street entrance of Central High.
>
> I parked my car about two blocks from the intersection. Newsom and I were in front with Hicks and Davy following, when we began the long, apprehensive walk.
>
> We had firsthand knowledge of where the nine stout-hearted Negro students were to enter; and we set off at a fast clip to be on hand when they arrived at the campus entrance.
>
> About midway of the final block, we picked up a tail of two whites. They made no comment. We kept moving forward.
>
> A crowd of about one hundred faced the school (away from us), waiting for the nine students to appear.
>
> Then, someone in the crowd of whites spotted us advancing.
>
> Suddenly the angry eyes of the entire pack were upon us. We moved forward to within ten feet of the mob. Two men spread their arms in eagle fashion. One shouted: "You'll not pass!"
>
> I tried to move to the left of the mob, but my efforts were thwarted. I made a half-turn left from the sidewalk and went over to a Little Rock policeman, who was standing mid-center of the street.
>
> "What is your business?" he asked. I presented my press card. He took his time checking it. Then he said: "You better leave. Go on across the sidewalk" (away from the mob at my heels).
>
> I followed his suggestion. After taking several steps, I looked back. The officer was near the opposite sidewalk, leaving the angry pack to track me.

CONTINUED

**Reproducible 3.10**
**Page 2 of 2**

The mob struck. I saw Davy being roughed up. Hicks and Newsom were retreating from kicks and blows. I stopped momentarily, as the boots and jeers behind me increased.

Strangely the vision of Elizabeth Eckford, one of the nine students, flashed before me as she with dignity strode through a jeering, hooting gauntlet of segregationists several days ago. Maybe, too, my training as a U.S. Marine in World War II and my experience as a war correspondent in Korea, and work on the Emmett Till case [a young African American boy who was lynched in Money, Mississippi, for whistling at a white woman] influenced my decision during that moment of crisis.

I decided not to run. If I were to be beaten, I'd take it walking if I could — not running.*

1. Why did Wilson refuse to run? What message was he trying to send? At whom was that message aimed? What individuals and experiences inspired his decision?

2. David Halberstam writes that however a reporter "feels about the events taking place in front of him, it has to be kept bottled up." What is Halberstam suggesting about the role of a reporter? To what extent do you think Alex Wilson would agree?

3. Why do you think Wilson and the other African American reporters found themselves part of the story rather than simply as reporters of the story? What is the danger in becoming part of the story?

---

* Will Counts *A Life Is More Than a Moment: The Desegregation of Little Rock's Central High.* Indiana University Press, 1999, pp. 49, 51.

**Reproducible 3.11**

## "Holding Up a Mirror"

David Halberstam was a young journalist in the 1950s. He has written about the dangers that reporters faced in Little Rock and how they responded to those dangers:

> Several *Life* magazine reporters were beaten badly by the mob early in the crisis, and then the reporters were arrested by local officials for having been beaten up. The [TV] network people, because of their high visibility, the familiarity of their faces, and the obvious presence of their cameramen, were particularly vulnerable. [TV reporter John] Chancellor soon found that when he walked down the street, he would often be followed by cars full of segregationists, hate contorting their faces as they stared at him. At first he would panic. *Should I run?* he would ask himself, but soon learned merely to keep walking. The locals became angrier and angrier — for television, in particular, was holding up a mirror of these people for the outside world to look at it, and the image in the mirror was not pretty.*

1. Study the photograph to the right carefully. How does it "hold up a mirror" for "the outside world to see"?

2. Melba Pattillo Beals writes that one Sunday she saw a "photograph of Elizabeth, walking alone in front of Central High on that first day of integration." The photo appeared in an ad paid for by a white man in a small town in Arkansas. The ad read, "If you live in Arkansas, study this picture and know shame. When hate is unleashed and bigotry finds a voice, God help us all." What do you think motivated the man to create the ad? How else might he have expressed his views?

3. If you were to create an ad using this photo, what would the ad say? To whom would you address the ad? What would the message be?

---

* David Halberstam, The Fifties. Fawcett Books, 1993, 681.

## Lesson 4: The Choices the Students Made

**Central Question:** How do the choices people make, individually and collectively, shape a society?

### Getting Started

Explain to students that this lesson looks at the choices made by students at Central High School during the 1957–1958 school year. You may wish to distribute **Reproducible 3.12**, a timeline of key events between September 25, 1957, and the end of the school year. For many students, it was a year like no other.

Only a small percentage of the white students at Central High School taunted or physically harassed African American students. The vast majority attended school each day and tried to avoid getting into trouble. Yet these students also made decisions that had important consequences. On the day the Little Rock Nine attended classes for the first time, Principal Jess Matthews issued a bulletin describing what he expected of Central High School students. The editors of the school newspaper also had ideas about how students ought to behave. Ask students to read both points of view on **Reproducible 3.13** and then work with a partner on their own list of ideas. Have partners share their ideas with the class. As students continue learning about the choices students made at Central High School, encourage them to revise or expand their lists. Ask them to also look for examples of good citizenship.

### Background Information

During the three weeks the nine African Americans could not attend school, they were tutored at the home of Daisy Bates, the president of the Arkansas NAACP. They also learned how to conduct themselves once school opened. Their parents and other adults in the African American community feared the nine would be taunted and harassed at school. Jim Lawson, a civil rights leader from Tennessee, met with the nine students and talked with them about the power of nonviolence. They were told that no matter what was said to them, they were not to retaliate. Responding to name-calling and other harassment would place all nine students in jeopardy.

The Little Rock Nine understood the importance of nonviolence but soon discovered how difficult it was to carry out — even with an armed guard. On Wednesday, September 25, soldiers from the 101st Airborne Division escorted the Little Rock Nine to school. A soldier accompanied each of the nine students to and from classes, but he could not prevent harassment in the classrooms, the cafeteria, the gym, or the washrooms.

In October, the soldiers of the 101st departed, leaving a federalized Arkansas National Guard in charge. By December, the harassment of the African American students had become more organized. The nine were finding themselves more and more isolated not only at school but also at home. Of the nine, Minnijean Brown was particularly vulnerable. Just before Christmas vacation, several white students constantly taunted her in the halls and hassled her in the cafeteria. She managed to ignore them for a time. Then one day, she retaliated by dumping a bowl of chili over two boys. She was promptly suspended from school.

### Activity: Creating an Identity Chart for Carlotta Walls

Distribute **Reproducible 3.14** and ask students to read an interview with Carlotta Walls, one of the Little Rock Nine. Then have students work with a partner to create an identity box or bag for her. What parts of her identity shaped the way she sees herself? What parts of her identity shaped the way others see her?

### Activity: Identifying Point of View (Big Paper)

Tell students that they will be discussing **Reproducible 3.14** in two stages. In the first stage, all communication will be in writing. In the second stage, they will have time to speak with their partners and the class as a whole. Try to give students time to ask questions before the activity begins to minimize interruptions later. Give each pair a large sheet of paper on which you have taped the following statement made by Carlotta Walls in the interview on **Reproducible 3.14**:

**"In my family, it was expected you would reach for an opportunity. This was a gold ring."**

Have partners read the quotation in silence and comment on the text and ask questions of each other by writing on the Big Paper. The written conversation must start with the text but can stray to wherever the students take it (including the identity charts). Allow at least 10 minutes for this part of the activity.

When time is up, ask students to leave their partner and silently walk around the room reading the other Big Papers. Allow enough time for students to not only read all of the other papers but also to comment on them in writing if they wish to do so.

When time is up, ask students to return to their own Big Paper. In this part of the activity, students are free to discuss the text, their own comments, what they read on other papers, and the comments their fellow students wrote on their paper. To conclude the activity, debrief the process with the entire class.

**Activity: Comparing Identity Charts**

Ask students to read **Reproducible 3.15** and create an identity box or bag for James Eison with a partner. How does he see himself? How do you think others see him? What seems to motivate the choices he made? After completing their chart, ask partners to compare it to the one they created for Carlotta Walls. How are the two charts similar? What differences seem most striking?

**Activity: Reader's Theater**

Explain to students that the Little Rock Nine had been warned not to respond to harassment at school. They were also told that they were not to come to one another's defense. It was too dangerous. To help them deal with the pressure, Ernest Green recalls, "We were visited and supported by a young divinity student from Vanderbilt University, Jim Lawson. Jim was a very strong supporter of Dr. Martin Luther King, Jr., and a student of nonviolence. It was his support and counseling that helped give us strength to endure each day. It was the feeling of faith, family support and the belief that we were doing the right thing that allowed us to look possible physical danger in the face each morning and not blink."

One day just before Christmas vacation, one of the Little Rock Nine did more than blink. Have students read **Reproducible 3.16** and discuss it briefly with a partner. Then have participants form a circle large enough to include everyone. Ask each student to read a sentence or two from the reproducible, going around the entire circle without stopping. (You may need to go around the circle more than once.)

Divide the class into groups of no more than six. Assign each group a passage of one or two paragraphs in length. Allow groups about 15 minutes to prepare an interpretation of their reading. Stress that the activity is an attempt to deepen the moment the writer is trying to convey. For example, one group may decide to do a choral reading (everyone reading in unison), or members may decide to have one person narrate while the others stand or move as appropriate. Have students consider using their voices in different ways or adding sounds to enhance the moment.

When groups finish their planning, form a large circle with everyone seated. Start with the group that has the first section of the reading. Go through the entire passage, one group at a time, with no pauses or breaks between groups. Have each group stand or sit in the middle of the circle as its members interpret their passage.

After groups have finished the reading, discuss:
- The choices various students made.
- How one or more of those students might have altered the outcome of the incident.
- What the students in the cafeteria learned from the experience.

**Activity: Expressing an Opinion**

Ask students to read **Reproducible 3.17**. It describes some of the choices white students made at Central High School. Have students work with a partner to identify the choice each made and the consequences of that choice. Ask students to list the ways those choices were similar. What differences do students notice among the choices and the consequences of those choices? Ask each student to write a paragraph that answers the question: How can one student make a difference? Remind students that their paragraph should include a topic sentence that expresses their opinion. The other sentences should contain reasons and evidence in support of that opinion.

**Activity: Last Word**

Ask students to give their impressions of graduation and what it means to be a graduate. Have students who have attended a graduation describe the ceremony. What does it mean to the graduate, to the parents, and to the teachers?

Explain to students that as the end of the school year approached, many people wondered if Ernest Green, the only senior among the now Little Rock Eight, would graduate. Would segregationists mount an attack during graduation? Ask students what they think will happen at graduation. Have them record their predictions in their journal or Interactive Student Notebook. Then distribute **Reproducible 3.18**.

After students have read Ernest Green's account of his graduation, explain that they will be discussing the following questions:
- What did Ernest Green accomplish?
- Why did he see that accomplishment as "cracking a wall"?
- What do you think it might take to tear down that wall?

Divide the class into groups of five and ask one person in each group to take no more than a minute to give their opinion on the first question. Then have each person in the group, one by one, respond to what the first person said and only what that person said in 30 seconds or less. When everyone has had a say, the first person to speak has the "last word." They can take 30 seconds to respond to the other speakers. To continue the discussion, ask a second person to lead a round of discussion on the second question. To conclude the activity, debrief the process with the entire class.

**Writing Suggestions**
- Review your list of suggestions for students at Central High School in 1957. What would you add to your list? Which suggestions would you like to delete? Which suggestions would you like to revise?
- Write a definition of good citizenship at school. What kinds of behavior mark a good citizen? What attitudes and beliefs are signs of someone who is trying to be a good citizen?
- What have you learned about choices and decision making from the experiences of the students at Central High School?

**Reproducible 3.12**

# Timeline

As you read and complete the activities in this part of the unit, highlight the events that you think are central to the story. Which event is a turning point in the story? A *turning point* is an event that marks an important change of course or an event on which important developments depend.

**September 25, 1957**   Federal troops escort the Little Rock Nine to classes at Central High.

**October 17, 1957**   Judge Davies dismisses a petition by the Mother's League to remove the federal troops who are in Little Rock in violation of state and federal constitutions.

**December 1957**   Taunted by white male students, Minnijean Brown dumps a bowl of chili on the boys harassing her in the cafeteria. She is suspended for six days.

**February 6, 1958**   Following additional confrontations with white students, Minnijean Brown is suspended by the Board of Education for the remainder of the school year. She transfers to New Lincoln High School in New York City.

**February 20, 1958**   The Little Rock School Board files a request for permission to delay integration until effective legal means exist for integrating the schools without impairing the quality of the educational programs.

**May 27, 1958**   Ernest Green becomes the first African American student to graduate from Central High School. He joins 600 senior classmates in commencement ceremonies as federal troops and city police are on hand.

**Reproducible 3.13**
**Page 1 of 3**

## What Should Students Do

Throughout the 1957–1958 school year, the principal of Central High School issued bulletins to students and teachers. The bulletin issued on September 25, 1957, read as follows:

This is the second bulletin to be read without discussion in your homeroom. Homeroom period will be extended till 9:05 this morning. Last night, the Federal Court ordered the Board of Education to begin today the integration of white and Negro pupils at the high school level, according to the plan of limited integration approved by that court and sustained on appeal. This Federal Court approved plan recognized the responsibility of the Board of Education to preserve the high quality of education in our schools. In order to carry out the directions of the Court, a group of qualified Negro pupils have been enrolled in Central High School this year. These students may be in attendance today, or at any future time. As a student in Central High School, you have certain duties to yourself and your school, and your community. You should know your responsibilities:

*You have a responsibility to yourself:*

a.  Your first and immediate job is to get an education of the highest quality possible. Any disorder, confusion, disagreement, or quarreling at or around school will interfere with classroom work. Such disorder, disorderly gatherings, or excitement *anywhere* will make it hard for you to study. For the sake of your progress in school, refuse to be drawn into any disputes or disputing groups.

b.  Any person interfering by word or action with the orderly carrying out of a direction from the Federal Court may be judged in contempt of that Court and will be subject to arrest and prosecution by the Federal Government. This is a serious offense and is punishable by fine, imprisonment, or both. Any name-calling, demonstrations, or similar disorder could be interpreted as contempt of court. This is no light matter.

*You have a responsibility to your school:*

Central High School has a reputation as one of the leading public high schools of the nation. It is important to each of us to keep it in that position. We can do that if each pupil and teacher will go quietly about our business here at school — learning and teaching. There must be no "incidents" at school.

CONTINUED

**Reproducible 3.13**
**Page 2 of 3**

*You have a responsibility to your city, state, and nation:*

The eyes of the nation and of the world are on our community during these days. The good name of our community will suffer if we become disorderly. How you or I conduct ourselves can help or hurt the reputation of our city, our state, and our nation. We can be known as law-abiding and peace-loving, or as quarrelsome and unintelligent. You and I can go about our business here and keep the headlines the kind that will make people want to live in Little Rock, Arkansas, or the U.S.A. — or we can make people scornful of our community as a place where people cannot manage to live peaceably.

From the cooperative expressions we have heard from numbers of our students, we are expecting the whole-hearted cooperation of our student body in these matters of importance to their individual records, to the good name of our school, and to responsible citizenship.

Jess W. Matthews, Principal

Georgia Dortch and Jane Emery, the co-editors of the Central High School newspaper, also expressed their views on how students ought to behave. On October 3, 1957, shortly after soldiers escorted the Little Rock Nine to school, the two girls wrote an editorial entitled "The Price We Pay."

On the 25th of September, with few words and fixed bayonets, crack paratroopers of the U.S. Army quickly dispersed the crowds that had gathered around Central and carried out the court order for integration. No violent incidents, as had previously occurred, were reported.

No matter what our personal opinions may be, we cannot be proud of the violence that occurred around our school that made it necessary for the use of these Federal troops. Looking back on this year will probably be with regret that integration could not have been accomplished peacefully, without incident, without publicity.

But the future remains.

And with the future remain many questions. Will there be more violence? How long will troop-protected education be necessary? Will our own educations be retarded?

The only answer to all these questions is for each individual to maintain a sensible, peaceful neutrality; to accept the situation without demonstration, no matter what personal views are entertained; and to make these, your years in Little Rock Central High School, the happiest and most fruitful of your academic education.

CONTINUED

**Reproducible 3.13**
**Page 3 of 3**

1.   How does the principal define good citizenship? How do the editors of the school paper define the term? How do you define it?

2.   With a partner, write your own set of suggestions for students at Central High School.

3.   What would you have written if you were the principal or the editors of the school paper?

**Reproducible 3.14**
**Page 1 of 3**

## "This Was a Gold Ring"

A Denver reporter interviewed Carlotta Walls LaNier about her experiences at Central High School. The story described the then 14-year-old's decision to attend the school.

Central felt like the natural choice....

"I was supposed to go to school there," LaNier said. "I passed it every day on the way to junior high school. I played baseball with the white kids all summer long. It seemed like a natural progression to go to school with them. No one expected all this.

"I knew it was important, but I didn't know what it would become," LaNier said. "I knew it was a step in the right direction. But I credit my parents for having those dreams — for having dreams and grasping opportunity."

She didn't tell her parents she was one of 147 black children to sign up to attend Central in the spring.

When the registration card arrived in July — along with a note to meet with the superintendent — it generated little discussion at home.

"In my family it was expected you would reach for an opportunity," LaNier said. "This was a gold ring."

The difference was stark between white Central High — hailed as the largest, most expensive, most beautiful high school in the nation when it was built in 1927 — and black Dunbar High — where LaNier would have gone to school and where her mother had graduated.

Central had 11,000 library books, compared with 5,000 at Dunbar. Central cost $1.5 million to build, Dunbar cost $400,000. Central had 100 classrooms, Dunbar 34. Central had science labs and athletic facilities. Dunbar had neither. The students at Dunbar received Central's hand-me-down textbooks.

CONTINUED

**Reproducible 3.14**
**Page 2 of 3**

"I knew when the white kids got new textbooks. It always made me happy because I knew we were going to get their old ones," LaNier said.

School Superintendent Virgil Blossom told the families of the 39 black children who eventually registered at Central that the students would be expelled if they retaliated against their abusers and, to minimize conflict, they wouldn't be allowed to participate in extracurricular activities. LaNier gave up student council and the basketball team. Others among the nine gave up track, choir and band.

"When you're going to school with all these opportunities and you can't take advantage of them, that's a little hurtful," LaNier said. "But we knew that going in."

After the meeting, the number of black students dwindled to 10. One girl didn't return after being confronted by the threatening mob the first day. The Little Rock Nine were born.

In 1957, Little Rock was a moderate Southern town in which whites and blacks generally got along.... But LaNier swam in a segregated pool. She was relegated to the balcony in the movie theater, was allowed at the zoo only on certain Lessons and often had to wait until she got home to use the bathroom.

LaNier was 11 when the *Brown* decision was handed down. "I knew how important it was," she said. "It was in our Weekly Reader in the sixth grade. It was reinforced in my elementary school and my church and my community. I knew what it meant — exactly."

She was excited by the prospect of her first day of school on Sept. 4, 1957, as she was every year.

"The first day of school was always a good day," LaNier said. "I had never missed a day of school since I started in the first grade."

That was about to change. As she arrived for her first day of high school, she was stunned by what she saw: a riotous crowd and National Guard soldiers brought in by Gov. Orval Faubus to deny them entrance to Central High, a school her grandfather, a mason, helped build....

Eight of the nine met at 13th and Park streets a block from school, where they were escorted by a group of supporters — NAACP leaders, ministers and rabbis.

The ninth, 15-year-old Elizabeth Eckford, didn't get the message and faced the jeering mob alone amid threats of lynching....

CONTINUED

**Reproducible 3.14**
**Page 3 of 3**

The nine returned to school three weeks later — on Sept. 23 — after a federal judge denied a school board request to suspend the integration plan. Television viewers nationwide watched as rioting broke out and the students were smuggled out a side door before noon. President Dwight Eisenhower, calling the rioting "disgraceful," ordered 1,200 members of the 101st Airborne Division to protect the children, and he placed the Arkansas National Guard under federal orders.

On Sept. 25 — the children's third attempt at a full day of school — they were escorted into Central by the soldiers. Each child was assigned a bodyguard.

A week later, the 101st Airborne turned over duties to the federalized Arkansas National Guard, and discipline problems broke out. The nine were harassed and intimidated. Gloria Ray was hit by a rock and pushed down a flight of stairs. Minnijean Brown was suspended for dumping lunchroom chili on antagonists and eventually expelled. Two white students were suspended for wearing cards that read, "One down ... Eight to go."

Carlotta Walls, whose heels were stepped on so often they bled, quietly made the honor roll.*

---

*Dave Curtin, "A Lonely March to Equality." *The Denver Post*, May 16, 2004.

**Reproducible 3.15**
**Page 1 of 3**

## "There I Was in History"

In 1997, reporter Ron Wolfe and Mary Hargrove interviewed Jim Eison for the *Arkansas Democrat-Gazette*. Eison was one of 50 white students who marched out of Little Rock Central High School on October 5, 1957, and crossed the street toward an effigy hanging from an oak tree. An effigy is a crude figure that stands for a hated individual or group. In this case, the effigy stood for the nine African American students. According to Eison, he and his friends did not know about the effigy in advance. The reporters describe what happened next.

> Some of the boys kicked and punched the straw-filled dummy that was dressed in blue jeans and an orange sweater. Rebel yells split the air amid shouts of, "Kill 'em, kill 'em!"
>
> One boy stabbed the dangling figure in the back with a penknife. Cameras snapped and whirred, and a photographer asked Eison what he was thinking. "Oh, if that were only a real one!" Eison cried.
>
> Someone set the effigy on fire, and it burned until the police pulled it down and stamped out the flames while the crowd booed.
>
> Seventeen-year-old Eison — the crew-cut son of a university professor — made national news that day. Maybe it was just Eison's luck that the cameras caught him. Maybe it was the shirt he was wearing, white with bluebirds, that grabbed their attention. Maybe he just said the wrong thing at the wrong time.
>
> "There I was in history," Eison remembers.

Although others have apologized for their behavior in 1957, Eison refuses to do so. The two reporters note:

> "I was a product of my day and time, and I was acting from my early upbringing," he says. Does it embarrass him now to be reminded what he said about the effigy? The question hangs for only a moment.
>
> "Of course, that's something I wouldn't say today, I assure you," Eison says. "Even if I felt that way, I wouldn't lower myself now to say something that crude.
>
> "The sentiment was true. I'd rather I hadn't said it, but at the same time I'm stubborn enough that I don't like people to make statements and then apologize. I think that's weak."

CONTINUED

**Reproducible 3.15**
**Page 2 of 3**

So he holds his ground. No polishing the scars off history.

No apology....

Oct. 3, 1957: Eison's memory is vivid as flame. These are moments, scenes he keeps ordered and tagged like museum treasures. He can minutely describe clothes, colors, hair, facial expressions, voice tones, the sound of boot cleats in the school hallways as soldiers marched the blacks to class.

The school world of 1957 is there for him like a painting under glass, all there with its white bobby sox and ankle-high pants, crew cuts, frocks, gloves, pretty blond girls and jeering hatreds.

He remembers how his "liberal" grandmother had angered him that year, telling him, "It's not going to hurt you to sit by them." Colonel Eison [his father] had warned even before, "Desegregation is coming whether you like it or not. It's coming."

But when it came, it hurt and scared the Eison boy in ways he couldn't name, and still can't.

"It challenged a way of life," he says. "Just how it was challenging, I don't know." But it threatened something so deep, so dear to him, that nothing good about desegregation could make up for the loss.

He describes a "beautiful middle-class existence" at 2411 Wolfe St., a 30-minute walk from the school. He was the only child of Colonel Eison, an engineering professor at the University of Arkansas at Little Rock, and Anna Bernice Reed Eison, a former teacher who owned Eison's Antiques.

"I had everything, parents at home, our house had beautiful antiques and a maid. I had every material thing you could want. And security," he says.

But not enough security, not enough protection to ward off this vague but awful change. Something — fate, life, time — *something* meant the end of life as he knew it, life steeped in white-columned images of the Old South and its grand codes of honor; something that ordered the South to move forward; something that didn't care how much the South yearned to go back. Something called desegregation.

Something had to be stopped.

Eison remembers, "We'd been warned not to walk out by the authorities, and we knew the world was watching at that time." The world was waiting just outside the school — waiting with cameras poised.

CONTINUED

**Reproducible 3.15**
**Page 3 of 3**

He didn't count how many other boys and girls joined the walkout. The news said 50 to 75, hardly a representative number of the 1,520 students attending that day. But it felt like a lot.

"People were cheering us on," he remembers. "Spectators — there were grown-ups. As you know, a lot of people came from the outside. I remember a lot of women. We walked down the front steps and went across the street.

"Someone had made this [effigy] and thrown the rope over the limb, and this one boy was hitting it and different people were throwing rocks. My best friend ran up with a pocketknife and stabbed it. And, boy, the photographers were taking pictures. Just click, click, click.

"I don't remember why this photographer turned to me, but he did and he said, 'How do you feel about it?' And that's when I said, 'Well, I wish he was a real one.'"

Eison also answered with his name and age, although "common sense would tell you not to do that," he says. "But I was carried away in the excitement. I felt like a big man. I was flattered by all the attention, I guess."

He walked out on school that day — past the assistant principal who was frantically trying to take names — in a show of "intense dislike" for blacks, and with practically no idea why.

"I didn't know anything about blacks," Eison says. "I didn't know anything about their history, what they had achieved or not achieved. Very few people did, either, very few.

"But the reason I maybe felt like I did — remember, I saw and observed these people on the streets, probably a lot of it came through my eyes. And then, another part of it probably came from peer pressure. A kid that age, you follow the crowd."*

---

\* Ron Wolfe and Mary Hargrove, "A Product of the Old South."© 1997 *Arkansas Democrat-Gazette.*

# The Chili Incident

**From *Warriors Don't Cry* by Melba Pattillo Beals.**

On Tuesday, December 17, when we had one more day to go before vacation, five of us entered the cafeteria. Lunchtime was always a hazard, and recently even more so. I had been avoiding the cafeteria, eating my sandwich alone in any safe place I could find. The cafeteria was such a huge place, with so many of our attackers gathered at one time. There were no official-looking adults or uniformed Arkansas National Guardsmen inside. Without fail, we knew we could expect some form of harassment.

As always on Tuesday the hot lunch was chili, which Minnijean loved. So while I took my seat with the others, she got in line to buy her chili. Ernie emerged from the line ahead of her and sat down at our table. As Minnijean made her way back toward us, her tray loaded down with a big bowl of chili, we saw her hesitate. She had to inch her way through a tight spot where mostly boys sat at tables on either side of her path. She had stopped dead in her tracks. We all froze, realizing she must be in trouble. We could see two boys near her — one directly in her path. Something awful was happening, but there was no way any of us could do anything to rescue her. We had been instructed that in such instances we were never to move toward the person in danger for fear of starting a riot.

I was panic-stricken. Minnijean was being hassled by those boys. Snickering among themselves and taunting her, they had pushed a chair directly in front of her. For a long moment, she stood there patiently, holding her tray high above their heads.

It was all I could do to hold on to my chair and not go to help her. Like a broken record, the words played over and over in my head — intervening on her behalf would blur the lines between who was the victim and who was the person at fault. If other white students joined the melee to rescue the other side, we'd have a brawl. They outnumbered us at least two hundred to one. Still, I wanted to go to her, move the chair, take her tray, tell her to back up and go another way, do something, anything.

As more and more people realized something was brewing, the chatter in the cafeteria quieted down. I could tell Minnijean was trapped and desperate, and very fast running out of patience. She was talking back to the boys in a loud voice, and there was jostling all around her.

CONTINUED

**Reproducible 3.16**
**Page 2 of 2**

Frantically I looked around to see if there were any adults nearby who could be trusted to help. We had come to believe that the vice-principal for girls, Mrs. Huckaby, made some efforts to be fair during these situations, but she was nowhere in sight. I beckoned to Minnijean to go around her hasslers, but she was standing perfectly still. It was as though she was in a trance, fighting within herself.

Later she would explain that the boys had been taunting her, sticking their feet in the aisle to trip her, kicking her, and calling her names. But we were not close enough to see details of the dilemma she faced. All we saw was her wavering as though she was trying to balance herself — and then her tray went flying, spilling chili all over two of the boys.

Everyone was stunned, silent for a long moment. Her attackers sat with astonished looks on their faces as greasy chili dropped down over their heads. All at once, our people who were serving food behind the counter began to applaud. This was greeted by an ominous silence and then loud voices, all chattering at once, as the chili-covered boys stood up. I wonder whether we'd ever get out of there alive. Suddenly a school official showed up, and Minnijean was whisked away, while we were hustled out of the cafeteria.*

---

\* Melba Pattillo Beals, *Warriors Don't Cry.*

## Can One Student Make a Difference?

At the beginning of the school year, Jane Emery, the co-editor of the *Tiger*, Central High School's newspaper, wrote an editorial that said in part:

> You are being watched! Today the world is watching you, the students of Central High....
>
> Will you be stubborn, obstinate, or refuse to listen to both sides of the question? Will your knowledge of science help you determine your action or will you let customs, superstition, or tradition determine the decision for you?...
>
> The challenge is yours, as future adults of America, to prove your maturity, intelligence, and ability to make decisions by how you react, behave, and conduct yourself in this controversial question. What is your answer to this challenge?

As you read about the various ways students at Central High responded to that challenge, use colored pencils to underline the choice they made and at least one consequence of that choice. Choose one color for the choice and a second color for the consequences or results of that choice. Which choices made a difference?

1. In 2004, Elizabeth Eckford sat down with CNN and recalled the events of the 1957–1958 school year at Central High School. When the reporter asked her about the atmosphere at school, she replied:

> We were physically assaulted every day. The principal's rule was that, no matter what was reported, he wouldn't act on any reports if a teacher didn't corroborate what we said happened. So, in essence, students had free reign to attack us every day. It was a coordinated group of about 55 students who attacked us out of 1,900 students at the school.
>
> A lot of people think, "We didn't know what was going on." People around me that I saw didn't react to what they saw or what they had to have heard. They turned their backs. It was impossible to have a friend. This was not anything like a normal environment. Anybody that would talk to us got a lot of pressure.
>
> There are two students I want to talk about that persisted in talking to me in speech class. Actually I was a very, very shy person, but I felt comfortable, felt that I belonged in that one class. At the end of the day, two people treated me like a human being (starts to cry). And when they just ... they persisted in talking to me every day like any other student. They didn't ask me something to see what "it" sounded like. They just talked to me.

CONTINUED

**Reproducible 3.17**
**Page 2 of 4**

I didn't know what happened to them. I knew something had to be happening to them. I didn't find out until 1996 what had happened to them. There was a boy and there was a girl. The boy was a senior, and there's a graduation picture of him standing next to Ernest Green and a bunch of students in the background looking at them and talking about them, just 'cause he was standing near Ernest Green.

But I found out in '96, because I had talked about these students over the years. In the '60s I started naming them. So, they had heard about me, and what it meant to me.

One girl named Ann Williams I found out didn't live in Little Rock. She said her family lived on a farm outside the city, and that her father had to hire armed guards for their home.

And the other student is Ken Reinhardt. Ken was harassed. He'd been knocked down, one time, he said, right in front of the gym teacher and the gym teacher did nothing.*

2. In an article entitled "Fear Is Portable," Terrence J. Roberts writes of his algebra class:
Algebra class was a haven for me. The teacher, Mrs. Helen Conrad, let it be known from the first day that she would tolerate no nonsense from anyone who opposed my presence. She was emphatic about it and the class responded accordingly. It was in this class also that I met Robin Woods, a white student who shared her textbook with me. Since my books and other school supplies were routinely destroyed by fellow students, I would come to class often with no supplies. Robin simply pulled her desk next to mine and we shared her book — an act that did not win her friends or favor. Her act of kindness was interpreted as a violation of the social code that outlawed any contact between black students and white students, especially black males and white females. Students who befriended any of the nine of us were labeled "nigger lovers" and shunned by those who wanted to preserve the old social order. Robin did not allow that kind of thinking to interfere with her choices.**

CONTINUED

---

* http://www.cnn.com/2004/LAW/05/17/eckford.transcript. Reprinted with permission.
** Terrence J. Roberts, "Fear Is Portable" in *President Dwight D. Eisenhower and Civil Rights*, http://www.eisenhowermemorial.org/DDEandCivil%20Rights-screen.pdf.

3. In her memoir, *Warriors Don't Cry*, Melba Pattillo Beals recalls a choice a classmate made on a cold day in March:

> As I stood alone outside the Sixteenth Street entrance of Central High, I was shivering against the cold, waiting for my ride home that Friday afternoon. I was immersed in fantasies about my quiet, safe weekend. My body was there, but my mind was somewhere else.
>
> Suddenly there was a voice in the distance, calling my name, jolting me from my thoughts. "It's nigger Melba." It was Andy's voice shouting at me. [Andy was a white student who harassed Melba.] My heart started beating fast. He was more than a block away, coming up from the playing field with a group of his friends. They were walking fast, almost galloping. Even if I started running, I couldn't out-distance all of them. I looked around frantically, searing for help.
>
> "Hey, Melba, you gotta get out of here." The second voice was much closer. I wasn't alone. There was a sleek, muscular boy, about six feet tall, wearing a varsity jacket and a cap, with a bushy shock of blond curls peeking from beneath it. He was leaning against the passenger side of a 1949 Chevy parked at the curb, only a few feet to my left. Was he one of Andy's friends, who'd come to corner me and hold me there? His face looked familiar to me. He resembled one of those big tough boys who got their kicks taunting me. But why wasn't he coming toward me, shouting ugly words like the others?
>
> "Nigger, nigger on the wall, who's the deadest of them all," Andy shouted as he hesitated, waiting for his friends. Now they were only about a quarter of a block away. "Stand still, don't run, 'cause if you do, it'll be worse for you," Andy shouted.
>
> What now? My mind scrambled to figure out what I should do.
>
> "Melba," the blond boy whispered my name, "listen to me. I'm gonna call you 'nigger' — loud. I'm gonna curse at you, but I'm gonna put my keys on the trunk of this car. Get out of here now. My name is Link, I'll call you later."
>
> "But I can't do that...."
>
> "You don't have any choice," he whispered. "Go!" I turned to see that Andy and his friends were only a short distance away. I wasn't even sure that I could make it to the car....
>
> "Hey, Andy, we're gonna have us some nigger tonight." I heard Link shout as he walked away from the car, toward them. I grabbed the keys and ran around quickly to open the door on the driver's side. I hopped in and locked all the doors.

CONTINUED

**Reproducible 3.17**
**Page 4 of 4**

> By the time I turned the key in the engine, Andy was clawing at the lock, while the other boys popped off the windshield wipers, and tried to get into the passenger's side. Link stood glaring at me with an anxious look on his face, spewing hate words just like them. I pressed down the clutch, shifted into first gear, and the car jumped forward. Andy was still running alongside, holding on to the door handle, but as I sped up, he had to let go.*

After that incident Link would often contact Melba to warn her of threats from his friends.

4. Jane Emery was a white student at Central High. She was the co-editor of the *Tiger*, the school paper. She wrote the editorial on page 1 of this reproducible. In a 1999 interview, she recalled a choice she made at the end of the school year:

> Towards the end of the year, graduation, Mrs. Huckaby [the vice principal of girls at Central High School] called five of us into her room … and she said … [during graduation] one of the five of us would be walking with Ernest Green. And so we could decide what we wanted to do, and Ernest understood if we were uncomfortable….
>
> There were five of us brought in … And I was the middle person, so of the five people, I would be the one, and so since they didn't know who was going to be absent, they would call five of us. And I didn't realize that I was going to be it. And I said, "I have no problem, I'll walk with him," and I really thought that was silly. And I didn't think anything about it.
>
> [Then] we started getting obscene phone calls [at] my home. My mother really got scared. I mean things like …"Are you a nigger lover, are you going to walk with him? You want your daughter to marry a nigger?" And it went on 'til late at night, and my mother took the phone off the hook, but she was absolutely scared to death, you know like the house was going to be blown up…. I was angry at the [whites] who did that, who really angered me. So, that just made me more determined that I was going to walk with him. And I walked with him, that was the first I ever talked to him."**

---

* Melba Pattillo Beals, *Warriors Don't Cry*. Abridged edition. Archway Paperback, 1995, pp. 171–172.
** Beth Roy, *Bitters In the Honey*. The University of Arkansas Press, 1999, p. 224.

**Reproducible 3.18**

## "I Had Cracked the Wall"

Ernest Green told an interview about his graduation:

> Graduation was the end of May. I had been there nine months and had thought that all I needed to do was graduate, just to get out of there, so that it would be impossible for white people to say that nobody black had ever graduated from Central High School. I was having difficulty with one course, it was a physics course, and almost up to the last minute I didn't know whether I was going to complete it successfully so that I would get out of there. But as things were, I got a fairly decent grade out of it.
>
> The interesting thing about graduation was, being the only senior, I'd given up all the graduation activity that had gone on in the black high school — the school play and the prom and all of those kinds of things. Sometimes because of not having that activity, I would really feel isolated, because I wasn't going to be at Central High School's prom, and I wasn't going to be invited to be in the school play at Central. But all of the black students at Horace Mann, which was the school I would have graduated from, invited me to all the activities, included me in all of it, really made me feel a super part of it. So I had the best of both worlds. I had cracked this white institution and still had all of my friends who were super-supportive of what I was trying to do.
>
> At the graduation ceremony, one of the guests was Martin Luther King. He was speaking in Pine Bluff, Arkansas, at the black college there. And he came up to sit with my mother and Mrs. Bates and a couple of other friends in the audience. I figured all I had to do was walk across that big huge stage, which looked the length of a football field. I'm sure it was very small, but that night before I had to walk up and receive my diploma, it looked very imposing. I kept telling myself I just can't trip, with all those cameras watching me. But I knew that once I got as far as that principal and received that diploma, that I had cracked the wall.
>
> There were a lot of claps for the students. They talked about who had received scholarships, who was an honor student, and all that as they called the names off. When they called my name there was nothing, just the name, and there was this eerie silence. Nobody clapped. But I figured they didn't have to. Because after I got that diploma, that was it. I had accomplished what I had come there for.*

1.     What did Ernest Green accomplish?
2.     Why did he see his accomplishment as "cracking a wall"?
3.     What was that wall? What do you think it might take to tear down that wall?

_____

* Henry Hampton and Steve Fayer, *Voices of Freedom.* Copyright ©1990 by Blackside, Inc. Used by permission of Bantam Books, a division of Random House, Inc.

# Lesson 5: The Choices the Community Made

**Central Question:** How do the choices people make, individually and collectively, shape a society?

## Getting Started

Minnijean Brown told a group of high school students a few years ago, "People make choices. There was no script for this event. Some chose to treat us the way they did and some people chose to sit by and do nothing." Students were not the only people who made choices in Little Rock during the 1957–1958 school year. Adults made decisions too. Explain to students that in this lesson, they will be examining a few of those choices.

## Background Information

Little Rock was considered a moderate southern city. Libraries, parks, and public buses had all been integrated without a fight. Yet, throughout the 1950s, life in the city was becoming more and more separate. The new neighborhoods that sprang up west of the downtown area after World War II were all-white communities. African Americans lived mainly in the east and southeast parts of the city. As the population on the west side grew, a new high school was built there. Hall High School opened as an all-white school the same year Central High School was desegregated. That decision angered many white families who lived in the Central High School district. They saw the new school as a way of protecting the wealthiest families in Little Rock from integration, while forcing it on middle-class and working-class white families.

The leaders of the segregationists included members of Little Rock's Capital Citizens Council (CCC) and the Mothers' League of Little Rock Central High School. Although neither group had more than a few hundred members, both were highly organized. They circulated petitions, organized phone trees, and blanketed the city with pamphlets and letters. They encouraged the violence with support from segregationists throughout the South. Most people in the city did not belong to these groups or to the mob that gathered outside Central High. Perlesta Hollingsworth is an African American who lived near Central High in 1957. In 1997, he told a reporter, "The shocking thing to me in 1957 was the number of whites who didn't participate in the aggression, who wouldn't do anything but look. Neighbors would express dismay, but wouldn't do anything, wouldn't speak out against it, would go ahead and close their doors to it."

**Activity: Categorizing Points of View**

Distribute **Reproducible 3.19**. Explain to students that it contains brief accounts of the various ways that adults in the community responded to the desegregation of Central High School. Have students work with a partner to label each decision and its consequences. They might choose to categorize people by the beliefs that shaped their decision (for example, segregation, integration) or by consequences of their choices (unites the community, divides the community, or resistance to change, acceptance of change). Discuss which decisions were easiest to categorize and which students found particularly challenging. What do the challenges suggest about the complexities of the choices people made? Which of the actions do students consider acts of good citizenship? What do those accounts add to our understanding of the term?

In the 1950s, many people in Little Rock and elsewhere considered themselves moderates. According to most dictionaries, a *moderate* is someone who does not hold extreme positions. Ask students which of the adults they read about would be considered people who held extreme views. Which would be considered moderates? Would their views be considered moderate today? Who decides what is an extreme position and what is a moderate one?

**Activity: Big Paper**

Tell students that they will be discussing **Reproducible 3.19** in two stages. In the first stage, all communication will be in writing. In the last stage, they will have time to speak with their partners and the class as a whole. Try to give students time to ask questions before the activity begins to minimize interruptions later. Give each pair a large sheet of paper on which you have taped the following statement by Perlesta Hollingsworth, an African American who lived near Central High in 1957:

> The shocking thing to me in 1957 was the number of whites who didn't participate in the aggression, who wouldn't do anything but look. Neighbors would express dismay, but wouldn't do anything, wouldn't speak out against it, would go ahead and close their doors to it.

Have partners read the quotation in silence and comment on the text and ask questions of each other by writing on the Big Paper. The written conversation must start with the text but can stray to wherever the students take it. Allow at least 10 minutes for this part of the activity.

When time is up, ask students to leave their partner and silently walk around the room reading the other Big Papers. Allow enough time for students to not only read all of the other papers but also to comment on them in writing if they wish to do so.

When time is up, ask students to return to their own Big Paper. In this part of the activity, students are free to discuss the text, their own comments, what they read on other papers, and the comments their fellow students wrote on their paper. To conclude the activity, debrief the process with the entire class.

**Activity: Expressing a Point of View**

Ask students to use the timelines in Part 3 to review the choices people in Little Rock and elsewhere made during the 1957-1958 school year. Then ask them to choose an individual or group of individuals who showed what it means to be a good citizen in a democracy and write a paragraph explaining their choice. Their answers should show an understanding of both citizenship and the roles individuals can play in shaping their community.

**Writing Suggestions**

- What does it mean to be a good citizen? What is the role of a citizen in a democracy?
- How did the silence of ordinary people give power to the mobs that gathered outside Central High School?
- Which of the choices you read about in Part 3 had the greatest impact on the outcome of events in Little Rock?

**Reproducible 3.19**
**Page 1 of 5**

## Categorizing Decisions

Adults, both Black and white, made decisions about the crisis in Little Rock. As you read about the various ways teachers, parents, and others in the community responded to events, use colored pencils to underline the choices they made and at least one consequence of that choice. Choose one color for the choice and a second color for the consequences or results of that choice. Then compare and contrast these choices with those you examined on **Reproducible 3.17**. What similarities do you notice? What differences do you consider most striking?

1. Daisy Bates, the president of the Arkansas NAACP, not only advised the Little Rock Nine but also served as their advocate. After Jefferson Thomas was physically beaten twice within a single week, she made a decision. She writes:

> After talking with Mr. Thomas, I checked my daily records. The boy who attacked Jeff had been repeatedly reported to school authorities for hazing the Negro students.
>
> At nine o'clock that morning, when Superintendent Blossom arrived at his office, Clarence Laws and I were waiting to see him. We asked him what he intended to do about the continued brutal attacks on the children by the organized gang — attacks that had been reported many times. He said he was not aware of a large number of repeaters. We showed him the record of the pupils who had taken part in various attacks. As he looked at the long list of names and the repeated brutalities against the nine children, his expression lost some of its hardness and his face seemed to soften. Momentarily there was no sign of the defiant attitude I had observed in him whenever anyone dared criticize him or his desegregation plan. Then as he straightened his shoulders, I said, "If you are really interested in clearing up this trouble, you should expel some of these repeated troublemakers."
>
> He looked at me and blurted, "You can't tell me how to run my school."
>
> "No, I can't," I retorted, "but it's up to you — not the Army — to maintain discipline inside the school. By not doing so, you are subjecting the children to physical torture that you will have to live with the rest of your life." As we left his office, I realized that we would have to seek help from some other source.*

CONTINUED

---

* Daisy Bates, *The Long Shadow of Little Rock: A Memoir.* David McKay Company, Inc., 1962, pp. 126–127. Reprinted by permission of the University of Arkansas Press. Copyright © 1987 by Daisy Bates.

**Reproducible 3.19**
**Page 2 of 5**

2. Daisy Bates writes:

> One day Gloria [Ray] started on her way down from the third floor of Central High School. She had taken only a few steps down the flight of steel steps when she heard a woman's scream from behind her. Gloria quickly connected the scream with some impending danger to herself. And she was right.
>
> A boy had silently been following her down the stairway. He was about to lunge at her to push her down the flight of stairs. The scream had alerted Gloria to the attack from behind....
>
> Many of the teachers — particularly the younger ones — did everything within their power to protect the nine students. Some went out of their way to help the students catch up with work they had missed when they were barred from entering the school in the first weeks of the term. Concerned over the lack of protection given the Negro students within the school, the teachers took it upon themselves to oversee the hallways in between class breaks. In this way they attempted to discourage the segregationist students from torturing the Negro children.
>
> One of the teachers had been standing in the doorway of her classroom looking down the stairway. It was she who had witnessed the attack on Gloria and had screamed the alert.*

3. Ann Tompson's parents made a decision soon after the school board announced plans to integrate Central High School. She recalls:

> My family were just ordinary, salt-of-the-earth people. My dad was a hardworking man who lived day-by-day, week-by-week. Although we were very poor, I didn't really know it. I felt as though I was the luckiest person in the world. Our life was very typical. Every day, I went off to school, my dad went off to work, and my mom worked hard at home. My parents' main concerns were making a living and raising their family.
>
> Segregation was simply the way of life; we never knew anything else. As it was in most southern cities, the blacks had their part of town, and the whites had their part. I can't remember ever going into a restaurant and seeing blacks there. I never really thought about it. My parents were wonderful people, but they were also a product of their society. We were all taught that you just don't mix. We were very ignorant about segregation and integration. It wasn't even an issue until we found out that they were going to integrate Little Rock Central High.

CONTINUED

_____
* Daisy Bates, *The Long Shadow of Little Rock: A Memoir.* David McKay Company, Inc., 1962, p. 144. Reprinted by permission of the University of Arkansas Press. Copyright © 1987 by Daisy Bates.

**Reproducible 3.19**
**Page 3 of 5**

I was a fifteen-year-old tenth grader when they made the announcement. At first, many of the parents refused to believe that it was actually going to happen. Some parents formed groups and committees to try and stop it, but my parents didn't really take part in any of that. It's not that they weren't interested; they just didn't know what to do or where to go. Ultimately, they just decided that their child was not going to an integrated school, and that was that. I don't think it was really out of hate for anyone. I think it was out of ignorance and fear of the unknown. "What would this lead to?" "What would be next?" That was the mind-set; people just didn't know what to expect. And we couldn't understand why they would ever want to leave their black school and come to Central in the first place.*

4. Daisy Bates writes:

When Governor Faubus was forced by the Federal Court to withdraw the Arkansas national guardsmen and to stop interfering with integration at Central High, [Eugene] Smith was Assistant Chief of Police. When school authorities wondered how they could protect the Negro students, Smith came to their aid. "Just give me the men and I will protect the children," he said.

When I was told to have the students assemble at my house by 8:15 a.m. on September 23, I asked who would protect the students. The reply was: "Smith, of course."

At 6 a.m. the next morning, facing a mob of one thousand, Smith stood with one hundred of the department's best men, blockading the streets to Central — a school he and his children had attended. Later, when the mob learned that the Negro students had gone inside the school, it surged against the police lines, ignoring Gene Smith's command to halt. One of the mob's leaders ran up to Smith and Smith knocked him to the pavement. Many were arrested and sent to jail.

… But when reporters questioned Smith on how he stood on the issue of integration, he replied, "That's out of my province. Our function is to do everything we can to protect life and property and preserve the public peace. And that's what we do every day."**

CONTINUED

---

\* Ann Thompson, "The Siege at Little Rock: Like the Civil War Revisited," in *The Century* by Peter Jennings and Charles Brewster. Doubleday, 1998, p. 353.
\*\* Daisy Bates, *The Long Shadow of Little Rock: A Memoir*. David McKay Company, Inc. 1962, pp. 182–183. Reprinted by permission of the University of Arkansas Press. Copyright © 1987 by Daisy Bates.

**Reproducible 3.19**
**Page 4 of 5**

5. Daisy Bates writes:

> Mr. [Dunbar] Ogden was a Southerner whose roots lay deep in the old plantation tradition: his heritage was linked to the slave-owning South. His great-grandfather, David Hunt, was said to have owned more slaves than any other man in Mississippi — and probably the South.... His father held a high ministerial post in the Presbyterian Church....
>
> The first time Mr. Ogden attracted my attention was when he was elected President of the Greater Little Rock Interracial Interdenominational Ministerial Alliance in June, 1957. It was this that led me to telephone and ask him to walk with the students to Central High School.
>
> When I talked to him that night, he was momentarily hesitant. "If it's God's will, I'll be there." Later he admitted that much of his hesitancy was due to simple fear. But much in his background and tradition also caused him to wonder and hesitate. "I was still thinking in terms of 'separate but equal,'" he explained. "I was incapable of a real relationship with Negro friends because I was still condescending in my attitude."
>
> The next morning, when the children assembled to go to school, Mr. Ogden was there to walk with them. With him was his son David. The father was pleased and proud that his son had accompanied him. "When I left the house this morning," he told me, "I wasn't sure how many would be here. I phoned all the ministers that I thought might come, but there was doubt in their voices. 'Isn't this a bit dramatic?' 'Is this the responsibility of the ministry?' In fact, more than one replied, 'I'm not sure that this is the will of God.' But as I was getting into the car, David came out of the house and said, 'Dad, I'll go with you. You may need a bodyguard.'"
>
> Only three ministers had come, and Mr. Ogden said somewhat apologetically, "I'm very discouraged that I wasn't able to get more, but frankly, I had to pray for courage myself. All I could think of was a pop bottle hitting me on the back of the head."
>
> He never suspected that the white citizens of Little Rock would turn on him. He was, after all, a minister and a Southerner. But that day, when he saw the stored-up hate in the mob and their contorted faces, when he heard them screaming not only for the blood of the nine Negro children but for his and all connected with him, he realized how vicious was the system under which he had lived all his life. "I became aware of where segregation led. I had to make a decision," he told me later....

CONTINUED

**Reproducible 3.19**
**Page 5 of 5**

To the segregationists, Mr. Ogden had become a traitor.... Members of his church stopped attending services, stopped giving financial support, and finally forced him to resign....

The night before Mr. and Mrs. Ogden left Little Rock ... they came to see me.... "I'm sorry I got you into this," I said.

He was silent for a moment. Then he said, "Don't feel sorry. If I had to do it all over again, I would. I believe that I'm a better Christian for having been privileged to participate in such a worthy cause."*

---

* Daisy Bates, *The Long Shadow of Little Rock: A Memoir*. David McKay, Company, Inc. 1962, pp. 189, 190–191. Reprinted by permission of the University of Arkansas Press. Copyright © 1987 by Daisy Bates.

# PART 4: The "Lost Year"

# PART 4: The "Lost Year"

## Central Question

- How do the choices people make, individually and collectively, shape a society?

## Student Outcomes

- Analyzes the choices individuals and groups made in response to the closing of every public high school in Little Rock
- Examines the role of the Supreme Court in a federal system
- Analyzes primary sources to identify point of view, attitude, and intent
- Uses logic and reason to defend a point of view
- Writes a persuasive speech, letter, essay, or other work

## Teaching Focus

Ernest Green's graduation did not end the crisis in Little Rock. In the school year that followed his graduation, the focus shifted from the classroom to the voting booth as the people of Little Rock voted on the future of their public schools and desegregation. Part 4 examines their decisions and the consequences of those decisions.

## Lesson 1: *The State v. the Federal Courts*

**Central Question:** How do the choices people make, individually and collectively, shape a society?

### Getting Started

Explain to students that Ernest Green's graduation did not end the crisis in Little Rock. As early as February 1958, the Little Rock School Board had asked the federal courts to delay integration until 1961. Not long after the school year ended, a district court allowed the delay. When the NAACP appealed the decision, the case eventually reached the U.S. Supreme Court. Ask students how they think the Supreme Court will rule and what effects that decision will have on Little Rock. What individuals and groups in the community are likely to play a leading role?

### Background Information

During the 1957–1958 school year, Little Rock became an increasingly divided city. Historian Tony Freyer writes that business activity slowed, as segregationists threatened and eventually carried out a boycott of shops and other businesses owned or run by moderates or supporters of integration. That is, they protested by refusing to buy goods or services from those companies. After years of steady growth, new industries abruptly stopped moving into the community.[12]

Governor Orval Faubus took advantage of the crisis and his new popularity. He now publicly criticized the federal government for creating a "police state" and openly attacked the Supreme Court. Many in Little Rock claimed that he was secretly helping segregationists in their efforts to remove the Little Rock Nine from Central High. Why was Faubus now so openly defiant? He was emboldened in part by the fact that the federal government had not prosecuted anyone who participated in the violence in Little Rock during the 1957–1958 school year — including those who tried to bomb the home of Daisy Bates. He was also aware of a letter a school board member had sent to President Eisenhower suggesting a meeting to discuss the question of "Where do we go from here?" Neither the U.S. attorney general nor the president responded. They had no interest in meeting with or actively supporting people who were directly involved in the crisis. Without federal support, many moderates in Little Rock came to believe that the only solution was to postpone desegregation. In February, the school board officially asked for a delay. On June 21, Federal District Judge Henry J. Lemley ruled in its favor. The NAACP promptly appealed the decision. On August 18, the circuit court of appeals overruled the decision by a six-to-one vote. The majority held that the threat of violence and related "administrative problems" do not affect a school board's constitutional responsibilities. The school board promptly appealed the new decision to the U.S. Supreme Court.

---

[12] Tony Freyer, *The Little Rock Crisis: A Constitutional Interpretation.* Greenwood Press, 1984, pp. 139–140.

**Activity: Analyzing a Timeline**

Distribute **Reproducible 4.1** — a timeline of events in Little Rock between February 1958 and September 29, 1958. Explain to students that the Supreme Court announced its decision on September 12, 1958, and promised to provide a written explanation of that decision no later than October 6. Remind students that Supreme Court justices watch TV, listen to the radio, and read newspapers and magazines. The justices knew what was happening in Little Rock. Have students highlight or circle events that might have been of concern to members of the court. How do students think those events may have influenced the justices' written decision? Have students work in pairs to identify three key events during this eight-month period. Ask partners to also identify one or more events that in their opinion mark a turning point in the crisis. A *turning point* is an event that marks an important change of course or an event on which important developments depend. Then ask each pair to write what they think will happen next in the story.

**Activity: Interpreting a Decision**

Distribute **Reproducible 4.2** — a summary of the Supreme Court's written decision and the reasons the court gave for that decision. Have partners underline the main ideas and then answer the questions at the end of the reproducible. Encourage students to use their answers to write a short news story about the decision. Their stories should answer the following questions:

- What question was the Supreme Court asked to decide?
- What are the facts of this case?
- What decision did the Supreme Court reach?
- Why is the decision important?

Remind students to include a headline that summarizes the main idea in 12 words or less.

**Writing Suggestions**

- Justices on the Supreme Court do not usually sign their opinions. All nine signed their decision in *Cooper v. Aaron*. Why do you think that they made a point of signing their names to the decision they made concerning the future of the Little Rock public schools?
- How do you think the court's decision will affect events in Little Rock?

**Reproducible 4.1**
**Page 1 of 2**

# Timeline

As you read and discuss this part of the unit, highlight the events that you think are central to the story. Which event marks a turning point in the story? A *turning point* is an event that marks an important change of course or an event on which important developments depend.

**February 20, 1958**    The Little Rock School Board asks the federal court for permission to delay integration.

**June 21, 1958**    Federal District Judge Harry Lemley grants a delay until January 1961. The NAACP appeals the decision.

**August 18, 1958**    The Eighth Circuit Court of Appeals in St. Louis overturns the district court's decision by a vote of six to one.

**August 21, 1958**    The school board appeals the decision to the Supreme Court.

**August 25, 1958**    The U.S. Supreme Court announces a special session to discuss the Little Rock school desegregation issue.

**August 26, 1958**    At Faubus's request, the Arkansas legislature passes bills that would allow him to close public schools to avoid integration and to rent the closed schools to private school corporations. Faubus delays signing the bills into law until the Supreme Court rules on the school board's appeal.

**September 12, 1958**    The Supreme Court rules that integration must continue. The justices announce they will give the reasons for their decision no later than October 6. Faubus signs into law the bills the legislature passed in August. The governor also calls for a special election on September 27 to decide whether the schools should integrate or close.

CONTINUED

**Reproducible 4.1**
**Page 2 of 2**

September 16, 1958    A group of white women who favor limited integration organize the Women's Emergency Committee to Open Our Schools. They are the first to challenge the governor by taking a stand against segregation.

September 19, 1958    Sixty-five white students at Hall High School issue a statement calling for the immediate reopening of their school even if it means admitting African Americans.

September 23, 1958    Governor Faubus asks the school board to turn its authority over Little Rock's public schools to a newly created private school corporation.

September 24, 1958    The NAACP challenges the constitutionality of the private school corporation.

September 27, 1958    Voters overwhelmingly oppose integration. At final count, 19,470 voted to close the schools rather than integrate. Only 7,561 voted to integrate.

September 29, 1958    The Supreme Court issues its opinion.

**Reproducible 4.2**
**Page 1 of 3**

## *Cooper v. Aaron*
## 358 U.S. 1 (1958)

Argued:     August 28, 1958
Decided:    September 12, 1958

### Facts of the Case

The Governor and the Legislature of Arkansas openly resisted the Supreme Court's decision in *Brown v. Board of Education*. They refused to obey court orders designed to implement school desegregation. Local officials delayed plans to do away with segregated public facilities.

### Question Presented

Were Arkansas officials bound by federal court orders mandating desegregation?

### Conclusion

In a signed, unanimous ... opinion, the Court held that the Arkansas officials were bound by federal court orders that rested on the Supreme Court's decision in *Brown v. Board of Education*. The Court noted that its interpretation of the Fourteenth Amendment in *Brown* was the supreme law of the land and that it had a "binding effect" on the states. The Court reaffirmed its commitment to desegregation and [repeated] that legislatures are not at liberty to annul [overturn] judgments of the Court.

CONTINUED

**Reproducible 4.2**
**Page 2 of 3**

In explaining its decision, the justices of the Supreme Court noted that they believed the School Board and the Superintendent of Schools acted in "good faith" during the 1957–1958 school year.

> We likewise have accepted the findings of the District Court as to the conditions at Central High School during the 1957–1958 school year, and also the findings that the educational progress of all the students, white and colored, of that school has suffered and will continue to suffer if the conditions which prevailed last year are permitted to continue.
>
> The significance of these findings, however, is to be considered in light of the fact, [that these] conditions … are directly traceable to the actions of legislators and executive officials of the State of Arkansas.… In its petition … the School Board itself describes the situation in this language: "The legislative, executive, and judicial departments of the state government opposed the desegregation of Little Rock schools by enacting laws, calling out troops, making statements [insulting] federal law and federal courts, and failing to utilize state law enforcement agencies and judicial processes to maintain public peace."…
>
> The controlling legal principles are plain. The command of the Fourteenth Amendment is that "no State shall deny to any person within its jurisdiction the equal protection of the laws." A State acts by its legislative, its executive, or its judicial authorities. It can act in no … other way.… In short, the constitutional rights of children not to be discriminated against in school admission on grounds of race or color declared by this Court in the *Brown* case can neither be [overturned] openly and directly by state legislators or state executive or judicial officers, nor [overturned] indirectly by them through evasive schemes for segregation.

The justices could have stopped at this point, but they chose instead to remind the governor and the legislature of their responsibilities under the U.S. Constitution.

> The Constitution created a government dedicated to equal justice under law. The Fourteenth Amendment embodied and emphasized that ideal. State support of segregated schools through any arrangement … cannot be squared with the Amendment's command that no State shall deny to any person within its jurisdiction the equal protection of the laws.… The principles announced in the [*Brown*] decision and the obedience of the States to them, according to the command of the Constitution, are indispensable for the protection of the freedoms guaranteed by our fundamental charter for all of us. Our constitutional ideal of equal justice under law is thus made a living truth.

CONTINUED

**Reproducible 4.2**
**Page 3 of 3**

1.  What are the facts of this case?

2.  What question was the Supreme Court asked to decide?

3.  What decision did the Supreme Court reach?

4.  Why is the decision important?

Use your answers to the questions above to write a short news story about *Cooper v. Aaron.*
Be sure to write a headline for your story. It should summarize the main idea in 12 words or less.

## Lesson 2: Shaping Public Opinion

**Central Question:** How do the choices people make, individually and collectively, shape a society?

### Getting Started

Until September 1958, only a handful of adults in Little Rock had openly expressed their views on integration. On September 27, every voter in the city had an opportunity to voice an opinion on the issue. Under a state law passed at the request of Governor Orval E. Faubus, Little Rock voters were given the choice of shutting down every public high school in the city or accepting the integration of all public schools in the city. A number of people in the community organized campaigns to sway public opinion. Ask students to think about some of the ways individuals and groups try to shape public opinion today. Which methods seem most effective? Which seem to be least effective?

### Background Information

Many historians believe that the 1958–1959 school year had a deeper and wider impact on the lives of residents than the confrontation between state and federal authorities in September 1957. In September 1958, voters in Little Rock were given the choice of shutting down the city's high schools or accepting the racial integration of all public schools in the city. They overwhelmingly voted to close the high schools to avoid integregation. That vote left several thousand students and their families scrambling to find alternative schooling in what many called the "Lost Year." During that year, many white students enrolled in private schools run by local churches. Hundreds of other students — including Melba Pattillo, Jefferson Thomas, and Terrence Roberts — left the city, and sometimes the state, to stay with relatives and friends so that they could finish high school. Others — including Elizabeth Eckford and Thelma Mothershed — took correspondence courses. Still others dropped out of school entirely.

As people in Little Rock realized that the schools would remain closed for the entire year, many parents searched for ways to reopen them. New groups were organized, and some existing groups reexamined their views on integration. A series of events provided opportunities for these groups to bring about change. In November, almost every member of the school board resigned. Desegregation was the only issue in the election that followed. This time, the city was evenly divided — three of the six seats went to segregationists and three to individuals who were willing to accept integration in order to reopen the schools. In March 1959, the Little Rock Chamber of Commerce announced its support for reopening the city's high schools even if it meant some integration.

In May, the three prosegregation members of the school board fired 44 teachers and administrators for supporting integration. Within days, residents of Little Rock formed a new group called STOP (Stop This Outrageous Purge) to recall the three segregationists on the school board. Segregationists responded by organizing their own group known as CROSS (Committee to Retain Our Segregated Schools). On May 16, STOP won a narrow victory. With about 25,000 votes cast, the three members of the board who supported segregation were removed by percentages ranging from 52.9 to 55.5 percent. Little Rock's high schools reopened in August 1959.

### Activity: Analyzing Political Ads

Explain to students that on September 27, the people of Little Rock had an opportunity to vote on integration. Both those who opposed integration and those who supported it tried to sway voters. Distribute **Reproducible 4.3.** Then give Packet A to half the class and Packet B to the other half. Have students work in small groups to analyze the ads. In analyzing an ad, cartoon, or any other message designed to persuade an audience, encourage students to:

- Look at the image or words and describe only what is on the paper. (There should be no interpretation at this stage.)
- Decide what emotion the artist or writer is trying to evoke.
- Determine what is the message. To whom is it directed? Is it a single message or will some interpret the work in other ways?

After students have had time to analyze their ads, have them share their findings with someone who examined the other packet. After partners have had an opportunity to discuss their packets, ask pairs to decide what kinds of political ads are most affective. What are the characteristics of a powerful persuasive letter or advertisement?

### Activity: Creating a Persuasive Message

Explain to students that when the votes were counted in September 1958, 19,470 voters chose to close the schools rather than integrate. Only 7,561 voted for integration. About six weeks later, five of the six members of the Little Rock School Board resigned. On December 6, voters went to the polls again — this time to choose a new school board. The choice was between candidates who favored segregation and those willing to accept integration if doing so would keep the schools open. Ask students to brainstorm how they might persuade voters to choose candidates willing to reopen the schools — posters, advertisements in local newspapers, speeches to civic and neighborhood groups, TV and radio commercials, fliers, etc.

Divide the class into small groups and ask each to design an ad campaign to elect board members who would work to reopen the schools. Depending on the class, you may wish to assign each group a particular campaign tool — a speech, flier, newspaper ad, TV commercial — or allow groups to choose the tool or combination of tools they think is most effective. Stress that projects will be evaluated on their appeal to a particular audience. How does the ad, speech, etc. persuade readers or viewers? Use **Reproducible 4.4** to help groups get started.

Have students use the criteria they developed in the previous activity to evaluate their efforts. Share with students the outcome of the December 6 election by distributing **Reproducible 4.5**.

### Writing Suggestions

- Rev. Colbert Cartwright of the Pulaski Heights Christian Church said of the "lost year," "In the end, the law could not do it. A group of very dedicated people — women,… marshaled … grassroots support to take back the schools and work on the desegregation problem. The lesson is that people themselves had to take responsibility for what they wanted their community to be.…They had to rally the good forces in the community to take back the schools, do more than a lackluster desegregation effort to abide by some edict. This was work that should have been done prior to desegregation." What do you think the lesson is?
- Many African Americans in Little Rock were voters, but they were not included in any of the groups that organized to open the schools. Why do you think Women's Emergency Committee and STOP chose not to accept African American members? How would you defend their choice? How would you challenge it?

Name _____   Class _____   Date _____

**Reproducible 4.3**

# Reading the Ads

Throughout the fall and winter of 1958, individuals and various groups in Little Rock created fliers, designed advertisements, and wrote letters and speeches. Each tried to sway public opinion on integration of the schools. As you examine each advertisement in your packet, try to answer the following questions about it:

1.  Describe what you see or read in the ad without trying to interpret it.

2.  Who authorized the ad?

3.  What emotion is the sponsor of the ad trying to evoke?

4.  What is the message?

5.  To whom is it directed? Is it a single message or will some interpret the work in other ways?

Advertisement in the *Arkansas Democrat*

A SPECIAL MESSAGE
ADDRESSED TO THE FOLLOWING
COLORED CITIZENS OF ARKANSAS

Dr. Lafayette Harris, President of Philander Smith College
Dr. J. M. Robinson, an outstanding doctor — leader and builder
Bishop Sherman
Reverend Guy
Reverend Roland Smith
Reverend Harry Bass
     All of whom are outstanding Christian Ministers

Dr. Harris, you are well aware of the fine cooperation, which has always existed in Little Rock between the races. With your great leadership, we (both white and colored) have built one of the outstanding colleges in the country.

This message is addressed to you and is being published in the press because you as leaders in your respective fields enjoy the respect and confidence of the people of your race as well as the white citizens of our state. Individually and collectively, you can make a great contribution and perform an important service in behalf of all citizens of our state in this grave situation, which has developed.

Until a year ago, the relations existing between the colored and white citizens of Arkansas were harmonious and pleasant. Each race respected and had confidence in each other. Down through the years, the colored and white citizens of Arkansas have accomplished much together for the good and improvement of all.

The key to the present grave situation which has developed and exists at this time, is in the hands of your race, the parents of the seven colored children and Mrs. L.C. Bates. The Federal Government, State Government and City Government have failed to furnish the leadership in this great crisis. As citizens of Arkansas and as leaders of your race, you are urged to counsel with those who direct the activities of the NAACP in Arkansas — parents of the children, recommend and urge that they be tolerant and not press their position too strongly at this critical time. Instead we urge you to induce the seven colored children to wait and give both you and us a chance to work this out in a peaceable manner. With time, we pledge with your help, we will solve this great problem.

SAVE OUR SCHOOL COMMITTEE
I. Smith, Secretary

**Small advertisements appeared in the *Arkansas Democrat.***
**Each was addressed to a leading white minister.**

BISHOP ROBERT R. BROWN

A trip to Washington won't help. Please appeal to Mrs. Bates and seven parents to give us time to accept this change in a Christian manner. Mrs. Bates holds the key.

> SAVE OUR SCHOOL COMMITTEE
> I. Smith, Secretary

---

BISHOP PAUL E. MARTIN

Please for all Christian people (white and colored) appeal to Mrs. Bates and seven parents to give us time and with men like you leading the way we can and will accept this change in a Christian way. Force and violence is not the way.

> SAVE OUR SCHOOL COMMITTEE
> I. Smith, Secretary

---

PREACHER DALE COWLING

You and your ministerial alliance please pray for Mrs. Bates and the seven parents to please give our Christian, law abiding citizens a chance to accept this philosophy in a Christian-like manner and not try to force us.

> SAVE OUR SCHOOL COMMITTEE
> I. Smith, Secretary

---

PARENTS AND TEACHERS

(Both white and colored) Please get petitions, rallies, and prayer meetings started to appeal to Mrs. Bates and the seven parents to give us time and we will help solve our problem in a Christian way, not by force, hate and violence. They hold the key.

> SAVE OUR SCHOOL COMMITTEE
> I. Smith, Secretary

**The Save Our Schools Committee issued the following statement in an advertisement that appeared in the *Arkansas Democrat*.**

Governor Faubus can't help us because he has a mandate from the people to stop forced integration and stop violence. (Faubus believes that the people make the law of the land.)

The federal government can't help us because they have a mandate from the NAACP to force this on us even with tanks, guns and bayonets.

If we can appeal to the parents of the seven children and Mrs. Bates and keep all outsiders out who started this thing, we can solve this problem in a Christian way with a little time. But force will not work; we freedom-loving, God-fearing American people will not bow down by force from anyone. Hitler, nor Hirohito [the leaders of Germany and Japan during World War II] could not make us knuckle under and neither can the NAACP.

We shall and continue to help our neighbors and brothers in a Christian way, but force never. The Communist and NAACP policy is divide and conquer; this is their first step.

## DO YOU WANT NEGROES IN OUR SCHOOLS?

IF YOU DO NOT THEN GO TO THE POLLS THIS COMING MONDAY AND

FOR REMOVAL **VOTE** AGAINST REMOVAL

LAMB
MATSON
TUCKER

McKINLEY
ROWLAND
LASTER

THIS IS THE SIMPLE TRUTH. IF THE INTEGRATIONISTS WIN THIS SCHOOL BOARD FIGHT, THE SCHOOLS WILL BE INTEGRATED THIS FALL. THERE WILL BE ABSOLUTELY NOTHING YOU OR WE CAN DO TO STOP IT.

## PLEASE VOTE RIGHT!!!

*Join hands with us in this fight— send your contributions to*

# THE MOTHERS' LEAGUE

P. O. BOX 3321 • LITTLE ROCK, ARKANSAS

Ad Paid for by Margaret C. Jackson, President; Mary Thomason, Secretary

1958-'59 — TEACHERS - NO STUDENTS | 1959-'60 — STUDENTS - NO TEACHERS

**Join With The Women's Emergency Committee to Open Our Schools**

NOT For Integration    NOT for Segregation    NOT Affiliated
with ANY other organization    FOR Public Education

Sign and Mail With Contribution to:
Womens Emergency Committee,
P. O. Box 177, Pul. Hts. Sta.
Little Rock, Arkansas
Ad Paid For By Mrs. Joe Brewer

Name ................................................
Address ............................................
City ..................................................

---

## It Is Time NOW To Say...

# STOP

Stop This Outrageous Purge

### STATEMENT OF PRINCIPLES

ADOPTED MAY 8, 1959, BY THE COMMITTEE TO

Stop This Outrageous Purge

In these principles we stand united:

1. We oppose the action taken by three members of the Little Rock School Board in attempting to discharge teachers without giving them notice or a fair and impartial hearing.

2. We believe the action of these three men constitutes a denial of basic rights to employees of our schools and will do irreparable damage to our public school system by destroying academic freedom and the faith of our teachers in themselves as free citizens.

3. We characterize the action taken by these three men as a purge which was cynical and designed to create a fear that stalks the classrooms.

4. The actions taken by Ben D. Rowland, Ed I. McKinley Jr. and Robert W. (Bob) Laster are a breach of public trust and justify their recall as members of the Little Rock School Board.

**Pick Up Your Recall Petitions Today**

1010 Pyramid Bldg.
9 A. M. to 5 P. M.

*Dial Information For Phone Number*

STOP

— MAIL TODAY —

STOP
1010 Pyramid Building
Little Rock, Ark.

I subscribe to STOP principles. You may use my name and enroll me as a member and accept this donation of $ ....................

Name ................................................

Address ............................................

Phone ............................ I will work—Call me.

Advertisement Paid For By Committee To Stop This Outrageous Purge, Drew F. Agar, Chairman.

**Reproducible 4.4**
**Page 1 of 2**

# Designing a Campaign

The focus of any election campaign is persuasion. Each side in Little Rock in 1958 had to convince voters to support its candidates. Whether your group creates an advertisement, prepares a TV commercial, writes a speech, designs a flier, or some combination of these approaches to persuade voters in Little Rock, you and your classmates will need to do the following:

**Choose a position.** What idea or issue do you want voters to think about when they go to the polls?

**Select an audience.** Decide if you are focusing on your base (people who agree with you) or you are trying to win over those who are neutral or those who disagree with your position.

**Support your position with evidence.** Persuasion requires convincing evidence. Use facts to support your ideas. Direct quotations from people who are respected or admired can also be persuasive. So can examples that enhance your ideas and make your topic come alive.

**Organize your project.** Figure out what you want to say and how you want to express that opinion. What is the best way to reach the people you want to reach? Be sure to take into account your goal, your audience, and your topic. You may also want to counter the arguments of opponents by providing contrasting evidence or by highlighting errors and inconsistencies in their logic.

## Guiding Questions

How can we get our audience's ATTENTION?
- Should we appeal to their senses with pictures, stories, music, humor, etc.?
- Should we appeal to their emotions with words or pictures that raise fears or evoke religious values or local pride?
- Should we appeal to people's intelligence with information, questions, stories, or displays?

CONTINUED

**Reproducible 4.4**
**Page 2 of 2**

How can we get our audience to TRUST us?
- Should we appeal to familiar ideas?
- Should we quote people who are admired, liked, or trusted?
- Should we use words that inspire trust (genuine, honest, sincere)?
- Should we include drawings or photos that inspire trust (smiling faces, voices that are reassuring, sincere looks, expressions)?

How can we MOTIVATE our audience to take action?
- Who is the audience?
- What is the audience seeking? Do people want relief? Protection? Prevention?
- What key words should we include to persuade people of the need to take action?

What kind of RESPONSE do we want from our audience?
- What words can we use to impress our audience with the importance of responding?
- Are there specific words we can use to encourage a specific response (voting, speaking, joining)?

**Reproducible 4.5**

# Timeline

| | |
|---|---|
| **September 1958** | As public high schools in Little Rock close for the year, 3,698 high school students have to find alternatives. |
| **November 12, 1958** | Five of the six members of the Little Rock School Board resign. |
| **December 6, 1958** | A new school board is elected with its membership evenly divided between those favoring compliance and those favoring resistance to the court's orders. |
| **March 1959** | Little Rock Chamber of Commerce votes 819 to 245 in favor of reopening the schools on a controlled minimum plan of integration acceptable to the federal courts. |
| **May 5, 1959** | Segregationist members of the school board try to fire 44 teachers and administrators suspected of favoring integration. The other three board members refuse to participate in the firing. |
| **May 8, 1959** | STOP (Stop This Outrageous Purge) is formed to recall the segregationist members of the board. Segregationists respond by forming CROSS (Committee to Retain Our Segregated Schools). |
| **May 25, 1959** | STOP wins the recall election by a narrow margin and moderates replace the three segregationists on the school board. |
| **June 18, 1959** | A federal court declares the state's school-closing law unconstitutional. The new school board announces it will reopen the high schools in the fall. |
| **August 12, 1959** | The school board opens public high schools a month early. Three African American girls enroll at Hall High School in west Little Rock. Jefferson Thomas and Carlotta Walls, two of the original Little Rock Nine, return to Central High for their senior year. About 250 protestors march to Central High. This time Little Rock police act quickly, arresting 21 and turning fire hoses on the remaining crowd. |
| **Fall 1972** | All grades in the Little Rock public schools are integrated. |

# PART 5: Legacies

# PART 5: Legacies

## Central Question

- What are the legacies of the choices citizens make, individually and collectively?

## Student Outcomes

- Analyzes the legacies of the crisis in Little Rock
- Analyzes primary sources to identify point of view, attitude, and intent
- Creates a monument or memorial that highlights the lessons learned from the crisis in Little Rock

## Teaching Focus

Part 5 explores the legacies of the *Brown* decision in Little Rock and elsewhere by focusing on the consequences of the decisions people made over 50 years ago. Unlike earlier parts of this unit, Part 5 contains a variety of articles and speeches that reflect on this period in history. Each offers a unique perspective. The central activity in the unit is the creation of a special project that showcases what lessons students learned from the crisis and what work remains to be done.

**Lesson 1: Legacies**                                                                                    149

> **Materials:** Reproducibles 5.1, 5.2, 5.3, 5.4, 5.5, 5.6, and 5.7
> **Activity:**  Remembering the Past

# Lesson 1: Legacies

**Central Question:** What are the legacies of the choices citizens make, individually and collectively?

## Getting Started

Ask students what lessons they learned from their study of the choices people made in Little Rock as a result of the Supreme Court's decision in *Brown v. Board of Education*. What lessons do they think the people of Little Rock learned from the crisis over desegregation? What did the nation learn? Have students record their ideas in their notebooks or journals.

## Background Information

Historian Taylor Branch has called the Little Rock crisis "the most severe test of the Constitution since the Civil War." In the more than 50 years since the *Brown* decision, much has changed in Little Rock and the nation. For example, although Central is still one of the nation's leading high schools, today it is an integrated school with an African American principal. While other cities in the country — both in the North and the South — have had more explosive racial problems over the years, Little Rock has continued to work toward uniting its people. It is also true, however, that much in Little Rock and the nation has not changed. Legal scholar Jamin Raskin notes that "in many parts of America, there are 100 percent white suburban schools and 100 percent Black or minority schools, and they are all perfectly lawful because the segregation is not commanded by the state."[13] In 1980, 63 percent of African American students attended mainly minority schools; by 1998, the figure was 70 percent.

## Activity: Remembering the Past

As a culminating activity, ask students to create a project that reflects what they learned from this unit about the way the government reacted and the role of ordinary citizens in that government. Their project could be a series of lessons that teach children, like the ones in Jane Elliot's classroom, about what it means to live in a diverse nation. Or students might design a monument or memorial. Remind them that a memorial does not have to be a building. It can be a website, mural, documentary, poem, story, or even a special service. These projects can be done alone, with a partner, or in small groups. In planning their project, students should begin by answering the following questions:
- What is the subject of your project?
- What do you want people to know or feel or explore?
- Whose story will be told and why?
- Who is your audience?
- What will visitors, viewers, or readers learn from the experience?

---

[13] Diana E. Hess, "Deconstructing the Brown Myth". *Rethinking Schools*, Spring 2004, p. 9.

Explain that Maya Lin considered these questions in creating a memorial to those who participated in the Civil Rights Movement. Encourage students to visit her memorial virtually by going to http://www.splcenter.org/crm/memorial.jsp and discuss how she answered each question. You may wish to point out that a Civil Rights Memorial Center is being constructed near the memorial. It will house exhibits on the Civil Rights Movement, a theater, and classrooms for educational activities. Ask students why they think the new building was needed. What will it offer visitors that they cannot learn from the memorial? You may also wish to have students visit www.facinghistory.org for examples of other memorials and/or to view monuments created by other Facing History students. Both sets of examples can be found in the Campus section of the website in the online module entitled "Memory, History & Memorials."

As students think about their project, you may wish to assign all or some of the reproducibles in this part of the unit (5.1, 5.2, 5.3, 5.4, 5.5, 5.6) to help think about the way various individuals and groups have thought about this history. One way to do so is by creating a jigsaw activity in which students read one reproducible and then share it with students who have read one of the other four.

Have students use the reproducibles and what they learned from this unit to design a project that reflects what they have learned from this unit about the role of government in a society or about civil rights and civic responsibilities. Each project should be accompanied by an explanatory paragraph. The paragraph should answer the following questions:

- What is the subject of the project?
- Whose story does it tell and why?
- Who is the expected audience?
- What will that audience learn from the experience?

You may wish to use **Reproducible 5.7** to guide the process.

**Reproducible 5.1**
**Page 1 of 2**

## What Has Changed? What Has Not Changed?

Joan I. Duffy, a reporter for the Little Rock Bureau of the *Memphis Commercial Appeal*, wrote in 1997:

> The Little Rock School Board voted to close the city's four high schools for the 1958–1959 school year, sending thousands of families scrambling to find alternative education for their children....
>
> No one knows how many students, unable to find an alternative school after the closure, dropped out and never came back. Newspaper accounts of the time described a rash of moving vans taking families out of Little Rock in search of schools.
>
> "Some 3,700 children of high school age have been affected by closings, 700 of them Negroes," a United Press International dispatch reported....
>
> Several churches cobbled together classes and a private, all-white school enrolled 917.
>
> Closing the schools and the "purge" of 44 teachers by the school board for perceived support of integration ignited the outrage of Little Rock's moderates. They were led by 76-year-old Adolphine Fletcher Terry, a civically active society matron who had organized the city's public library system. She organized an army of 2,000 women — all of them white. By spring of 1959, a recall movement ousted three segregationists from the school board and replaced them with moderates. The schools re-opened in the fall of 1959.*

Rett Tucker, the president of the Chamber of Commerce, told Duffy, "Historians say that was the end of it, but you and I know we've been dealing with it ever since." *U.S. News & World Report* revealed some of what the school, the city, and the nation have been "dealing with" ever since.

> In some ways, Central High stands as a model of desegregation's success. The once all-white student body is now 58 percent black and 39 percent white. The school produces many of the state's brightest students, black and white, and sends them on to the nation's best universities. Over the past decade, of Arkansas's 32 black National Merit semifinalists, 15 have come from Central High....

CONTINUED

---

* Joan I. Duffy, "A Reunion with History: Central High Will Observe 1957's Rite of Passage" *Memphis Commercial Appeal*, September 21, 1997. Excerpt used with permission.

**Reproducible 5.1**
**Page 2 of 2**

At Central High School, the honors classes are mainly white. The regular classes are primarily African American. No one seems sure why this is so. Some think it is due to racism. Others attribute it to the poor academic preparation of incoming Black students. The article goes on to note:

> The racial makeup of classrooms reinforces self-segregation in other parts of school life. Many black students walk or take the bus to school and enter through the school's front doors. Most white students drive cars and come in a side door near the parking lot. Most black students eat lunch inside, near the hot lunch line, while white students eat outside, near the concession stand. And even though most Central High students generally say they have friends of different races, they acknowledge that for the most part they hang out with friends from their neighborhood, their junior high, or their classes.*

1. How has Central High School changed since 1957? How has your school and others in your community changed since 1957?

2. In what respects has Central High School stayed the same?

3. What is self-segregation? How is it like the segregation of the past? How is it different?

4. What part does race play in segregation? In self-segregation? How do both shape identity?

———————

* Copyright 1997 *U.S. News & World Report*, L.P. Reprinted with permission.

**Reproducible 5.2**

# Little Rock Nine Recognized for Heroism

In 1999, each of the Little Rock Nine received the Congressional Gold Medal, Congress's highest civilian honor for their "selfless heroism" during the crisis atmosphere of 1957. At a White House ceremony to mark the occasion, various individuals commented on the award. As you read their comments, decide whose views are closest to your own. If you had been at the ceremony, what questions would you have asked? What would you have wanted guests to know?

### Ernest Green

"The last 42 years represent a commitment that none of us had any idea would result in this. We were really ordinary people…. It has been a long journey, but I think each of us would consider it worthwhile. While the sacrifices have been great, we recognized in 1957 that it was not an easy journey."

### Former Arkansas Senator Dale Bumpers

"A lot of people do laudable things, and some people do sort of brave things, but very few people do truly historic things — and heroic. These nine children were asked to be both brave and heroic, and they were. Their place in history is finally etched and will never be erased."

### President Bill Clinton

"[These nine teenagers] taught us that you can turn your cheek from violence without averting your eyes to injustice. And they taught us that they could pay their price and go on."

### Arkansas Senator Tim Hutchinson

"The nine gave meaning to the Constitution. They quietly but resolutely persevered, and their courage forced this nation to come to terms with the incongruity [absurdity] of revering the Declaration of Independence while simultaneously denying the fundamental truth that all men are created equal."

### Arkansas Senator Blanche Lincoln

"There is no question in my mind that my life is more productive because of what you did…. Thank you for having the personal fortitude to endure so people like me could come behind you."*

---

* *Arkansas Democrat-Gazette*, November 10, 1999.

## Remembering the Past

In 1997, a Central High School Visitor Center opened across the street from Central High School in an old gas station. A reporter described the center:

It features exhibits about the confrontation between Faubus and Eisenhower and about the campaign of abuse waged against the black students once they entered the school. Students were regularly spat upon and body-slammed into lockers. Broken glass was left on shower floors.

The exhibit also includes a black-and-white photograph of Ernest Green, the only senior among the Nine, in his cap and gown at his graduation ceremony, where the announcement of his name was greeted with silence. It concludes with a color photograph of smiling students at last year's highly integrated commencement.

The nine former students are now spread across the world. They are writers and accountants and professors and real estate agents....

Daisy Bates, the NAACP leader who served as a mentor to the students, still lives in the house where the students gathered in the weeks they were prevented from going to school. Though a stroke has slurred her speech and limited her hearing, she remembers the events of 40 years ago with clarity.

"I knew by going through this that it would help the children of that time and the children of this time too," said Mrs. Bates, now in her 80s.

Because the history is still so raw, and because many of the participants are still alive, the commemoration makes many here uneasy. Some black residents fear that it may close a chapter prematurely. Some whites dread the rehashing of memories that they would like to see buried.

Craig Rains, a member of Central's Class of 1958 and now a prominent public relations consultant, left town for three days this month after *The Arkansas Democrat-Gazette* reprinted a page from 1957 that quoted him declaring his support for segregation.

Rains underwent something of an epiphany [a sudden realization or understanding] after watching his classmates verbally abuse Ms. Eckford during the first week of the integration crisis. He now lives in a racially mixed neighborhood and serves on the commission planning the commemoration.

Joan Adcock, another white member of the class and now a member of the Little Rock City Board, worries about the classmates whose children and grandchildren may see them in unflattering photographs at the visitor center.

CONTINUED

**Reproducible 5.3**
**Page 2 of 2**

"We shouldn't have to be responsible in our 50s for things we did as teen-agers," Ms. Adcock said. "We grow up. Some of those people have come forward publicly and said how ashamed they are."

[Melba Pattillo] Beals, one of the Little Rock Nine, does not buy that rationale. "Their grandchildren might see who they were back then and then celebrate their growth," she said. "What would they have us do, deny that it happened?"

Today's Central High students are acutely aware of the history of their school, and many attribute its academic achievements to an intense motivation to overcome the past.

"We take the torch we got from the Little Rock Nine and we pass it from class to class," said Ms. McKindra, the student body president.

She and other students said that race relations were congenial at the school but that blacks and whites divided up in social settings. White students, for the most part, eat lunch at picnic tables outside. Black students, for the most part, eat in the cafeteria.

"There was a pep rally last week and I looked up at the seniors, and all the whites were sitting together and all the blacks were sitting together," said Derrick Floyd, a black senior and star basketball player. "I said to myself, 'Why aren't we all sitting together?'"*

1. Who or what do the exhibits at the Visitor's Center commemorate and why?

2. What is the purpose of the exhibits?

3. Whose story is told and why?

4. Who will visit the center?

5. What do visitors learn from the exhibits?

6. What would you add to their learning? What lessons would you stress?

7. How would you answer the question Derrick Floyd raises at the end of the article?

**Reproducible 5.4**
**Page 1 of 3**

## President Bill Clinton's Remarks

On September 25, 1997, President Bill Clinton spoke at Central High School to mark the 40th anniversary of the integration of the school. As you read, underline the way he answers the following questions:

- Who is he honoring and why?
- Whose story is he telling?
- What has he learned from his story?
- What does he want his audience to learn from the story?

Forty years ago, a single image first seared the heart and stirred the conscience of our nation. So powerful, most of us who saw it then recall it still. A 15-year-old girl, wearing a crisp black and white dress, carrying only a notebook, surrounded by large crowds of boys and girls, men and women, soldiers and police officers. Her head held high, her eyes fixed straight ahead. And she is utterly alone.

On September 4, 1957, Elizabeth Eckford walked through this door for her first day of school, utterly alone. She was turned away by people who were afraid of change, instructed by ignorance, hating what they simply could not understand.... Elizabeth Eckford, along with her eight schoolmates, were turned away on September 4th, but the Little Rock Nine did not turn back. Forty years ago today, they climbed these steps, passed through this door and moved our nation. And for that, we must all thank them.

Today, we honor those who made it possible, their parents first. As Eleanor Roosevelt said of them, to give your child for a cause is even harder than to give yourself. To honor my friend Daisy Bates and Wiley Branton and Thurgood Marshall, the NAACP and all who guided these children.

To honor President Eisenhower, Attorney General Brownell and the men of the 101st Airborne who enforced the Constitution; to honor every student, every teacher, every minister, every Little Rock resident, black or white, who offered a word of kindness, a glance of respect or a hand of friendship; to honor those who gave us the opportunity to be part of this day, a celebration and rededication.

CONTINUED

**Reproducible 5.4**
**Page 2 of 3**

But most of all, we come to honor the Little Rock Nine. Most of those who just watched these events unfold can never understand fully the sacrifice they made. Imagine, all of you, what it would be like to come to school one day and be shoved against lockers, tripped down stairways, taunted day after day by your classmates, to go all through school with no hope of going to a school play or being on a basketball team, or learning in simple peace....

But let me tell you something else that was true about that time. Before Little Rock, for me and other white children, the struggles of black people, whether we were sympathetic or hostile to them, were mostly background music in our normal, self-absorbed lives. We were all, like you, more concerned about our friends and our lives day in and day out. But then we saw what was happening in our own backyard, and we all had to deal with it. Where did we stand? What did we believe? How did we want to live? It was Little Rock that made racial equality a driving obsession in my life....

Well, 40 years later we know that we all benefit, all of us, when we learn together, work together and come together. That is, after all, what it means to be an American. Forty years later, we know, notwithstanding some cynics, that all our children can learn, and this school proves it.

Forty years later, we know when the Constitutional rights of our citizens are threatened, the national government must guarantee them. Talk is fine, but when they are threatened, you need strong laws, faithfully enforced, and upheld by independent courts.

Forty years later we know there are still more doors to be opened, doors to be opened wider, doors we have to keep from being shut again now.

Forty years later we know freedom and equality cannot be realized without responsibility for self, family and the duties of citizenship, or without a commitment to building a community of shared destiny, and a genuine sense of belonging.

Forty years later, we know the question of race is more complex and more important than ever, embracing no longer just blacks and whites, or blacks and whites and Hispanics and Native Americans, but now people from all parts of the Earth coming here to redeem the promise of America.

CONTINUED

**Reproducible 5.4**
**Page 3 of 3**

Forty years later, frankly, we know we are bound to come back where we started. After all the weary years and silent tears, after all the stony roads and bitter rods, the question of race is, in the end, still an affair of the heart.

But … if these are lessons, what do we have to do? First, we must all reconcile [settle our differences]. Then, we must all face the facts of today; and finally, we must act.…

And what are the facts?

It is a fact, my fellow Americans, that there are still too many places where opportunity for education and work are not equal, where disintegration of family and neighborhood make it more difficult.…

There is still discrimination in America.

There are still people who can't get over it, who can't let it go, who can't go through the day unless they have somebody else to look down on. And it manifests itself in our streets and in our neighborhoods, and in the workplace, and in the schools. And it is wrong. And we have to keep working on it, not just with our voices, but with our laws. And we have to engage each other in it.…

We have to decide … all you young people have to decide, will we stand as a shining example or a stunning rebuke to the world of tomorrow? For the alternative to integration is not isolation or a new Separate but Equal, it is disintegration.

Only the American idea is strong enough to hold us together. We believe — whether our ancestors came here in slave ships or on the *Mayflower*, whether they came through the portals [gates] of Ellis Island or on a plane to San Francisco, whether they have been here for thousands of years, we believe that every individual possesses a spark of possibility.…

… We must be one America. The Little Rock Nine taught us that.…
We have to act. All of us have to act, each of us has to do something, especially our young people must seek out people who are different from themselves and speak freely and frankly to discover they share the same dreams.

**Reproducible 5.5**

## Governor Mike Huckabee's Remarks

On September 25, 1997, Arkansas Governor Mike Huckabee also spoke at Central High School to mark the 40th anniversary of the integration of the school. What idea does he emphasize in his speech?

Some have asked: how long are we going to deal with this Central crisis situation? Are we going to have to relive it every few years? ...

Well, let me tell you how long we will deal with it — until justice is the same for every human being whether he or she is black or white, we will deal with it. Until the same rules apply to get a bank loan for every person regardless of who he or she is, we will deal with it. As long as there are whites who turn around and see a black person coming and bring fear to their hearts, we will deal with it. And as long as there are blacks who look and see and have resentment toward a white person, we will deal with it. We will deal with it until the dream of Dr. Martin Luther King lives in all of our hearts, and that is that we will judge people by the character of their hearts and not by the color of their skin....

Today, as we dedicate the Little Rock Central Visitor Center, I will tell you that last Friday my daughter and I went there. We walked through that exhibit and it brought memories to me of the time when Sarah was 11 and we went through Yad Vashem in Jerusalem to visit that incredible place that is dedicated to the memory of the victims of the Holocaust — another one of our history's horrors. And as we went through Yad Vashem, she saw the pictures of the horrible treatment and of the extraordinary injustices of the evil that was marked by that time. I never will forget when we came to the end of that exhibit and there at the guest book ... was a space for comments.

As long as I live I will remember as my daughter paused and then wrote words that will forever be in my mind. She wrote simple words. I wondered as we went through it, did she understand the message of it, did she get it? If there was any doubt, it was erased as I looked as those words. Because those words simply said, "Why didn't somebody do something? Why didn't somebody do something?"

In silence, we left and I knew she got it. Today, as the world once again revisits Little Rock and the great state of Arkansas and its great people, I hope that never, ever, ever does someone have to ask why didn't someone do something. As for those who go through that visitor center and may ask why didn't someone do something, I hope they will take a good, long look and realize that today we celebrate nine people who did do something.

**Reproducible 5.6**
**Page 1 of 3**

## Did the *Brown* Decision Make a Difference?

In 2004, Americans marked the 50th anniversary of *Brown v. the Board of Education.*
*Teaching Tolerance* interviewed a number of prominent people about the legacies of *Brown.*
One of the questions was: **Are students better off today than before *Brown v. Board?*** As
you read a few responses, think about how they apply to you, your school, and your community.

**Cheryl Brown Henderson**, a daughter of the late Reverend Oliver Brown, the namesake of
*Brown v. Board of Education*

> Yes, all people have in some ways benefited from this decision. Although issues of
> achievement persist, they are born largely from poverty and schools within certain
> areas that lack basic resources to accommodate students whose backgrounds have left
> them behind in terms of preparation for formal education.
>
> It requires a greater investment of teacher talent, fiscal resources, access to technology,
> mentors and individualized attention to close the gap for students in this situation.
>
> Ultimately the *Brown* decision afforded all citizens more choice and freedom in
> their daily lives. *Brown* set legal precedent for other cases heard by the Supreme
> Court as well as civil rights legislation (that) focuses on race and gender equity.

**Reg Weaver** is a former middle school science teacher and president of the National
Education Association.

> The opportunities to learn are certainly broader today than in 1954. We have made
> progress in boosting the academic achievement of African American students.
>
> Between the mid-1970s and the end of the past century, black high school students
> raised their graduation rates to 80 percent and increased their college enrollment rate
> by more than 40 percent, and they had the single largest improvement of any ethnic
> group in reading scores on the National Assessment of Educational Progress, the
> nation's report card.
>
> Educational possibilities have opened up not just for African American students,
> but also for all students regardless of color, gender, income, geography, special needs,
> native language, or immigration status.
>
> School integration has enriched the educational experience of all of our children
> by teaching them to understand and appreciate diversity.

CONTINUED

**Reproducible 5.6**
**Page 2 of 3**

Even though [segregation] in our schools is dead, the reality is that millions of African American, Hispanic, and other minority children still go to segregated schools and receive an education inferior to that received by most white children. Many schools in urban and rural areas are in critical condition — buildings are crumbling and overcrowded, too many teachers are uncertified, class sizes are too large, and student achievement is dismally low.

Several years ago, I did an exchange between my students in Harvey, Ill. and students in a public school in a wealthier Chicago suburb called Naperville. My students were shocked to learn what the Naperville school had: air conditioning, no water pipes breaking, clean bathrooms that work, security, a gym, a nice cafeteria. And when these children finished visiting this terrific school and community, they asked me, "Do we have to go back where we live? Why can't our school and neighborhood be like this?"

At suburban schools across the country, children of every race and ethnicity walk through the same front door. But, too often, they walk down different corridors — and sit in separate classrooms. Too often, minority children find themselves in special education and non-college-bound classes. Many minority students are still not graduating with diplomas and are dropping out of high school in disproportionate numbers. For many children, the reality is still separate and unequal....

Are students better off today? In many ways, yes, but we still have not fulfilled the promise of *Brown* by providing every child the opportunity to attend a great public school.

**Juan Williams**, journalist and author of *Eyes on the Prize: America's Civil Rights Years, 1954–1965*. Today black and Latino students live in a different America than the nation that existed at the time of *Brown*. The nation's neighborhoods and public schools are more segregated in many areas than they were before *Brown*.

In the big cities, especially in the Northeast and the Midwest, there is a far higher number of black and Hispanic students. At the same time, white families and their children have left urban neighborhoods and schools. The result is that most black and Latino students are in schools that are made up of mostly minority students. In addition, the schools under the most pressure to deal with poverty's impact on children are usually those minority-dominated schools in the cities.

CONTINUED

**Reproducible 5.6**
**Page 3 of 3**

But I would argue that even those students are better off than before *Brown*. Spending on those schools is far higher than the spending on segregated black public elementary and secondary schools before *Brown*.

The cultural acceptance of inferior schools for black and brown children is gone. Americans know this is wrong. The problem is that people close their eyes. But legal action and public policy arguments rage today over how to improve those schools. That is why the controversy over vouchers, charter schools and the use of magnet schools is at the center of any discussion of public education in America today. In addition, don't forget the public schools outside those big cities. Hispanic and black students are in those schools today. Fifty years ago their attendance would not have been possible.*

---

*This essay originally appeared in *Teaching Tolerance* magazine (*Teaching Tolerance*, no. 25, Spring 2004). Reprinted with permission.

**Reproducible 5.7**

# Planning a Project

In planning your project, you may wish to work alone, with a partner, or in a team. Begin by deciding what individual, idea, or event you would like to remember and why.

If you decide to build a monument:

- Sketch possible ideas for your monument on paper or in clay. You may want to research possible images for your monument before choosing a design.
- Once you have decided on an appropriate design, choose the building materials for your monument and select an appropriate site for the completed work.
- Build a three-dimensional model of your monument and then write a short essay explaining the concept behind your monument and the process involved in creating it. The following questions may help you organize your thoughts:

   What is the title of the monument?

   What prompted you to create this particular monument?

   What are the ideas underlying your monument?

   Describe the details of your monument that your think are the most powerful or important.

   Where would you like your monument to stand? Why did you choose this setting?

   How do you hope people will respond to your monument?

Share your essay and your monument with your classmates. Discuss the process as well as the final product. What did you learn about yourself and the memories that shape your identity?

If you decide to build a website or an exhibition, write a story or a poem, or create a set of lessons, the process is similar:

- What is your main idea? What do you want people to know, experience, or feel?
- Brainstorm ways that you can share that idea with others.
- Once you have decided on a project, decide on the elements that you will include in it. For example, if it is a set of lessons, how will you divide them? What will you teach first, second, and so on? If it's a website, what stories or images will it include? How will users navigate the site?
- Create a rough draft of your project. Ask friends to look it over and make suggestions. What can you do to make it more powerful? More interesting? Easier to read?
- Create your project and then write a short essay explaining what prompted you to create this particular project. How do you hope people will respond to it?

Printed in the USA
CPSIA information can be obtained
at www.ICGtesting.com
JSHW052146081023
R12999000001B/R129990PG49632JSX00001B/1